THE ART OF MENTORING

For a complete list of Management Books 2000 titles,
visit our web-site at http://www.mb2000.com

THE ART OF MENTORING

HOW YOU CAN BE A SUPERB MENTOR

MIKE PEGG

2000

Copyright © 1999, Mike Pegg

First published 1999 by Management Books 2000 Ltd,

Forge House, Limes Road
Kemble, Cirencester
Gloucestershire GL7 6AD
Tel: 01285-771441/2. Fax: 01285-771055
e-mail: m.b.2000@virgin.net

Printed and bound in Great Britain

British Library Cataloguing in Publication Data is available

ISBN 1-85252-272-0

CONTENTS

INTRODUCTION

How can you be a good mentor? How can you pass on your wisdom? How can you help people to find their answers to challenges?

Great mentors help people to take more control of their lives and find their own way to fulfilment. What happens in a mentoring session? This introduction gives a snapshot of one meeting which followed the classic 'Five C' model. It shows how to help people to focus on their Challenges; Choices; Consequences; Creative Solutions; and Conclusions. The following pages provide a road-map for running a structured session. You can, of course, follow the route in your own way.

Stephen enjoyed a job few of us would envy. He was the Director of an Assessment Centre for the 'criminally insane.' Pressure from politicians called for him making daily decisions about life or death.

"My job is to decide whether murderers, rapists and others can be released back into the community," he said. "If we get the judgement right, nobody knows about our efforts. If we get the judgement wrong, the newspapers call for my head."

Decision day loomed for Stephen. Two years previously he had been head-hunted to lead the Assessment Centre at a notorious Special Hospital for violent criminals. He now faced several problems. First: The boss who recruited him had promised complete autonomy, but she had now left. Political forces had taken over. The Government was 'advising' Stephen to make the right 'political decisions' before the General Election, saying: "Dangerous people should not be released onto the streets." Second: His diary was filled with Whitehall meetings dominated by bureaucratic infighting. Stephen had little time left to devote to his patients and do the work he loved. How to find answers to these issues?

CHALLENGES

"Can you fax me the topics you would like to discuss," I asked Stephen a week before our meeting. Within 24 hours he sent the following list:

- How to use my talents to make my best contribution to society?

- How to manage political pressure?

- How to regain satisfaction in my work?

Meeting at a hotel near Heathrow, we began the 3 hour session by finalising the agenda. Where did he want to start? Stephen opted to tackle his top challenge.

"How can I make my best contribution to society?" he asked. "If we solve that problem, everything else will fall into place. Money is nice, but I want to feel alive in my work, not half-dead."

CHOICES

Drawing on the flip-chart, Stephen outlined the five possible options he had been considering:

a) Remain in his job as head of the Assessment Centre.

b) Get a similar job in another Special Hospital for the criminally insane.

c) Become a consultant.

d) Take early retirement.

e) Do something completely different.

MENTORING MODEL

**Mentors help people
to focus on their:**

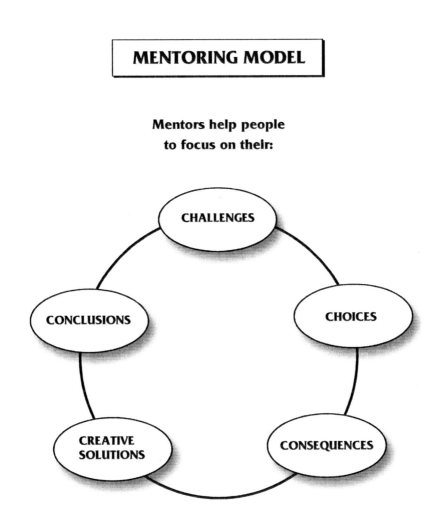

"Strange as it may sound, I like working with the patients," he said. "Maybe I'm mad, but I feel it is a job that benefits the community. Patients are often easier to manage than the bureaucrats and politicians."

CONSEQUENCES

Stephen and I then explored the pluses and minuses of the possible options. For example:

Option A: Staying in his role as head of the Assessment Centre.

Pluses: Contributing to society; working alongside dedicated colleagues; excellent money; tempting pension.

Minuses: Government interference; endless meetings; loss of integrity.

Thirty minutes were spent highlighting the consequences of pursuing the five different routes. Stephen then moved on to the next step.

CREATIVE SOLUTIONS

Good mentors are fine listeners, but sometimes they must step beyond the role of being a 'Third Ear'. Mentees are hungry to explore new ideas for achieving their picture of perfection, which is where mentors earn their corn.

"Peak performers build on their strengths: so what do you do best?" I asked Stephen. "When creating fine work, they balance apparent contradictions. They see, for example, both the big picture and the small details. Do you ever juggle such paradoxes? Re-visiting our positive history can provide the key to finding future fulfilment. What successful projects have you completed in the past?"

"I am an entrepreneurial psychiatrist," said Stephen. "Encouraging people is my vocation, but I also like to make a 'profit'. My talent lies in finding money to provide niche services. Ten years ago I started a Counselling Service for companies. Seven days a week we provided telephone and face-to-face counselling for employees facing problems. Autonomy is in my blood, however, rather than taking orders from bureaucrats."

Stephen did not shout 'Eureka!', but he quickly saw another creative road. He could set-up a company supplying the Government with outside Assessment Services for the criminally insane. The Pluses: Doing work he loved; picking a team of professionals; building a business that served society. The Minuses: Financial risk, but this could be minimised; dealing with key Government players, but this could also be managed. Accepting the whole package, he said: "Let's do it."

CONCLUSIONS

Feeling a sense of urgency, Stephen began writing his business plan. Starting from his destination and working backwards, he created the following picture of his goals.

In 2 Years Time I Intend:

- To have contracts that bring in £500,000 per year.

- To supply Assessment Services to three major Special Hospitals.

- To have a team of five excellent professionals who can market, sell and deliver Assessment Services.

- To have a full financial back-up plan, including insurance covering professional litigation, that provides security against potential hazards.

- To have written three articles that have been accepted by respected medical journals. Publishing will help to establish our credibility.

Two years was a long time: so what must he begin doing tomorrow? Stephen compiled a list that included: Making a clear contract with his employers; contacting potential customers in other Special Hospitals; selling the benefits of an outside Assessment Service to the Government.

One year has now passed since meeting Stephen, who fought to overcome some initial resistance. Government service proved tougher to leave than anticipated. Bribed with an increased salary, he negotiated a phased withdrawal and six months later started his own business. Annual contracts have been agreed for supplying Assessment Services to two Special Hospitals. Determining the future of dangerous people, he is making an invaluable contribution to our society. Feeling alive, he is now making full use of his talents. Stephen is developing through tackling the next fulfilling challenge in his career.

How can you develop your mentoring skills? This book provides a framework that you can use to enable people to find answers to challenges. It is divided into three chapters.

1) THE PHILOSOPHY OF MENTORING

How to clarify your core beliefs? How to start out as a Mentor? How to build credibility? How to define what you can and can't offer as a Mentor? How to get the right balance between 'Pulling' and 'Pushing'? Beliefs shape our behaviour. This chapter provides exercises you can use to clarify your philosophy as a Mentor.

2) THE PRINCIPLES OF MENTORING

How to facilitate a session as a Mentor? How to mentally rehearse what might happen? How to focus on the real results the person wants to achieve? Taking you 'inside' a meeting with a business leader, this chapter provides trigger questions you can ask at each stage of the Five C Model. Written in an in-depth style, it outlines the principles you can follow to enable a person to tackle difficult problems.

3) THE PRACTICE OF MENTORING

How to use exercises to bring the session to life? How to work with different kinds of people? How to use the model with teams? Written in a journalistic style, this chapter describes meetings with a sales-person, a soccer player and the senior team of a small company. Some readers may prefer to start by exploring this practical chapter and then move back to the theory.

Great educators create a 'stimulating sanctuary'. Mentors take a similar approach. They help people to build on their strengths, find solutions and achieve ongoing success. Please take the ideas you like best in this book and use them to pass on your knowledge to future generations.

Note: The names of people and companies mentioned in this book have been changed to protect their identities. Some of the reported speech has also been summarised. I have tried, however, to be true to the spirit of the work and provide tools that people can use as Mentors.

1

THE PHILOSOPHY
OF MENTORING

MENTOR WANTED

- Must be both warm and wise

- Must be able to both gain credibility and make people feel comfortable

- Must be able to be challenging and also guide people to finding creative solutions

- Must be both sage-like and street-wise

- Must be able to create a demand for their services as a mentor

You are unlikely to see this advert when visiting the Job Centre or reading *The Sunday Times*. So how do you become a mentor? The mystical answer is: "When the mentor is ready, the mentee appears," but what happens in practice? How does your first mentoring job appear? Ann runs her own Executive Mentoring company. How did she get started? Her answer is typical.

"Somebody asked me," says Ann, who jokingly calls her company 'Rent-A-Mentor. "I'd run two Top Team workshops for a high tech company. The MD said he wanted to talk alone with me about some issues facing the business. Meeting off-site for three hours, we explored the challenges he faced. He found the session useful and this led to individual meetings with several other directors. The pattern was repeated with two other companies, both of whom pay me on a retainer basis. Virtually all of my time is now devoted to Executive Mentoring."

Imagine you want to pursue a path similar to the one travelled by Ann. How can you gain credibility? How can you be a good sounding board? How can you pass on your knowledge in a way people can accept? One way to start is defining your philosophy of mentoring. Imagine you were searching for somebody to help you to find solutions to challenges. What qualities would you look for in such a person? Try tackling the exercise called *My Ideal Mentor,* set out opposite. One person wrote, for example:

MY IDEAL MENTOR WOULD BE:

- Somebody who I could respect.

- Somebody who made me feel safe.

- Somebody who I could bounce ideas off.

- Somebody who helped me to find creative solutions to problems.

- Somebody who encouraged me to act, rather than to talk too much.

Mentors come in all shapes and sizes. You often hear a soccer player, actor or business leader, for example, describe somebody they met in the past by saying: "They acted as a mentor for me." Mentors play many different roles. So what's the difference between, Mentoring, Teaching, Advising, Coaching, Counselling, Modelling and Leading? Let's explore some of these different approaches.

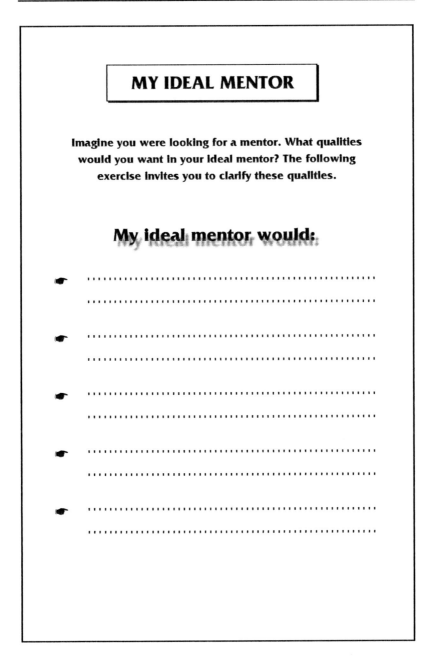

MY IDEAL MENTOR

Imagine you were looking for a mentor. What qualities would you want in your ideal mentor? The following exercise invites you to clarify these qualities.

My ideal mentor would:

☛ ....
....

☛ ....
....

☛ ....
....

☛ ....
....

☛ ....
....

THE MENTOR'S MANY ROLES

CLASSIC MENTORS

Mentors are 'wise and trusted advisers'. They have credibility and are willing to pass on their wisdom. Giving an overview of the jungle, they outline the roads people can follow towards achieving their picture of perfection. Sage-like and street-wise, they share their knowledge in a way that helps people to take greater control of their lives.

MODELS

Models are people that we admire. They provide examples that we may wish to copy and emulate. Teachers, for instance, can have a profound impact on us if they are inspiring and bring their subject to life. Sometimes we find ourselves talking, dressing or acting like them in our own lives. Positive Models at work, for example, teach us about 'the things you must do to be successful around here.'

TEACHERS

Great teachers share their knowledge and make learning enjoyable and effective. They focus on the Three I's: Inspiration, Implementation and Integration. First: They inspire people to want to learn. Second: They provide implementation tools that work. Third: They help people to integrate the learning into their daily lives. We never forget a great teacher.

ADVISERS

Advisers are people we seek out to obtain specialist knowledge. Mentors can move into the role of providing advice, but everything must be above board. Why? They are changing the rules of engagement. Positioning what they are about to say, for example, they can state: "If it is okay with you, I am now going to step out of my role and just give you a straight piece of advice." Mentees can then apply the same judgement criteria as with any professional advisor. Mentors must not 'slip into' giving advice without first making clear contracts with the person on the receiving end.

COACHES

Coaches work with people on a daily basis. They educate them to upgrade their skills as, for example, a soccer player, engineer or therapist. Good coaches often take three steps. First: They encourage people to build on their strengths. Second: They equip people to tackle areas for improvement. Third: They enable people to achieve ongoing success. Good coaches recognise that people have different learning styles. Before communicating knowledge, they ask themselves: "How can I put this message in a way the person can accept?"

COUNSELLORS

Counsellors meet people who want to solve a problem they are experiencing in their personal or professional lives. The classic method is to create a warm climate, practice listening skills and be non-directive. Providing the Counsellor acts as a good 'Third Ear', the person is often able to find their own answers to problems.

'BUDDIES'

The 'Buddy System' is used by some organisations. Experienced staff members are assigned to new employees to 'show them the ropes.' Much depends on the quality of the Buddy. 'Old hands' can teach the newcomer to be positive or negative, to develop good habits or bad habits. Buddies are sometimes called Mentors, but they are mainly concerned with helping the newcomer to feel at home.

LEADERS

Leaders are people who inspire us to do our best. They come in all shapes or sizes. Wartime heroes, for example, do not always succeed during peace. Great leaders reach the heart as well as the head. They encourage us to focus on certain values, pursue a clear vision and deliver visible results. Robert Greenleaf's writing on *Servant Leadership* offers an insight into the qualities that can bridge the gap between leadership and mentoring.

Mentors may switch between the various roles. Is this okay? Yes, but with one proviso. Ethics underpin everything. Clear contracting is crucial, so you may say: "If it is okay with you, I am now going to step into a different role." Confidentiality requires, of course, that the topics discussed remain between the two parties. Ethics may also lead you to choose to work with people in some professions and not in others. "To thine own self be true," is the time-honoured advice. Mentoring is most satisfying when you are fully committed to helping the other person to find fulfilment.

How to get your first client? "Twenty years elapsed before anybody formally asked me to be their mentor," said Ann, "Like in any vocation, I served a long apprenticeship." One approach is to focus on the Three C's: Credibility, Clarity and Customers. Let's explore these foundations for sharing your knowledge.

CREDIBILITY

Mentors start by gaining respect. How? Different people adopt different methods of establishing authority. Sir John Harvey-Jones, for example, won admiration for his leadership at ICI. Executives were then delighted to be filmed taking his advice in the BBC TV series *Troubleshooter*. Here are some ways that individuals earn credibility.

THROUGH AGE

Grey hair equals wisdom. Mentors find it helps to be older than the mentee, perhaps because we all grew up wanting to respect our parents and teachers. George Mead's writing on 'Significant Others' shows how we seek models to admire. Age also brings accountability. Certainly I got a shock when, aged 40, I ran a workshop for the Directors of a high tech company. Suddenly realising I was the oldest person in the room, I felt increased responsibility for the ideas I was sharing.

THROUGH BOOKS

Authors gain respect by publishing books. "Consultants are ten-a-penny." said one Managing Director. "My board will only listen to people who take the trouble to package their know-how." Rosebeth Moss-Kanter and Tom Peters, for example, have reached business leaders by publishing best-sellers. Not everybody can sell a million copies, but putting a book on the table is more impressive than mass-mailing a brochure.

THROUGH KNOWLEDGE

'Mad professors' speak rapidly, firing ideas as if spraying the audience with a machine gun. Why do we listen? Somewhere we may find golden nuggets. Professor Tom Cannon, author of *Welcome To The Revolution*, certainly isn't mad, but his lectures offer listeners a stunning tour-de-force journey through the annals of business history. Leaving the audience breathless, he gains respect for his intellect and quick-fire brain.

THROUGH SUCCESS

"Soccer is a results business," said one club manager. "Discussing soccer problems, I take advice from managers who have won trophies. Everybody has opinions, especially about who to pick in the team. I only listen to people with a track record of winning championships."

A similar rule applies in most fields. Famous hoteliers, film directors and scientists, for example, start with an advantage when opening their mouths. A word of warning. Brilliant practitioners seldom make great teachers. Many have employed their natural talent to reach the top. Sometimes they get impatient with students, stating: "Look, it's so obvious, just do it." Stars can find it difficult to share their knowledge. Past glories buy them time, however, as admirers are awe-struck in the presence of greatness.

THROUGH STREET-WISDOM

Sally was 28 years old when she became the youngest board member in a travel company. She took the alternative route – rather than the academic route – to success. Leaving college with few paper qualifications, she spent three years as a holiday rep in the Mediterranean. Gaining rave reports from customers and colleagues, she returned to take a sales job at head office in London. Top sales performer for three successive years, she then moved into Human Resources and transformed the sleepy outpost. Sally is now sought out by rising stars. She is seen as street-wise and knowing her way around the system.

THROUGH CHEMISTRY

"Dave is the only outside adviser we employ," said the MD of a leading-edge company. "Why? Two reasons. First: He immediately 'Got It' when I walked him around the building. The chemistry was right and he quickly understood our culture. Second: He had the courage to stand up to my senior team, who eat consultants for breakfast. Continuity is vital in our culture. Dave spends half a day with every new manager. Acting as a confidential outsider, he explains the 'rules' for achieving success in our company. Why? Directors must not abdicate responsibility, but newcomers welcome the chance to talk with someone impartial. Dave has helped us to retain five talented managers who might have walked to our competitors in Silicon Valley."

THROUGH BEING A TRUTH-TELLER

Managing Directors are frequently fed a censured picture of reality. Colleagues speak in 'code'. Pausing for a moment, they alter their language to be diplomatic, or to obscure, what is really taking place in the business. Mentors gain respect by giving an honest picture. Truth-tellers must be tough yet tactful, because the first reaction to bad news may be denial. The art is to communicate in a way that enables people: a) To see what is happening. b) To see positive solutions. Reality checks provide the foundation for achieving success. Every MD needs a Truth Teller. Who plays this role in your business?

THROUGH EXPERTISE

Credibility comes through establishing authority in a specific subject: Be it architecture, bee-keeping, creativity, dancing, education or whatever. What is your niche? One marketing company, for example, hires an actress to coach its presenters in voice technique. She is savvy enough to stick to her speciality, however, and avoids wandering into giving opinions about the company's financial strategy. Choose an exhilarating vocation and become an expert in that particular field.

THROUGH PRESENCE

Mother Teresa transmitted this quality. Wrapping you in her spell, she made you feel special. Presence does not call for jumping around a stage giving inspiring speeches. Derek, a Human Resources Director, has an almost Zen-like authority. His diary is packed with meetings staff invite him to attend. Why? Caring and calm, Derek creates a sanctuary where people feel they can open their hearts and minds.

THROUGH APPEARANCE

Tall and beautiful people attract attention, but not everybody can be a basketball player or model. Dress can, however, be crucial. Executive Mentoring calls for wearing a well-tailored suit, for example, rather than gardening jeans. (Unless that is the dress code on the day.) Dressing appropriately fulfils two functions: a) To feel comfortable yourself. b) To minimise any 'interference' so that people can hear your message.

Mentors win respect in different ways. How can you gain credibility? Several tips are worth bearing in mind. First: Be true to yourself. Second: Be clear on your strengths. Third: Be clear on your limits. (A topic we will explore in the next section.) Try tackling the exercise called Credibility, opposite. Describe three things you can do to build respect as a Mentor. Let's move on to the next stage of preparation before setting out on your journey.

CREDIBILITY

Different mentors gain respect in different ways. What are your strengths? What other things can you do to make sure that people are open to what you offer? Describe three things you can do to gain credibility as a mentor.

1) I Can ....
....
....

2) I Can ....
....
....

3) I Can ....
....
....

CLARITY

"Clarity is vital," advised Ann. "Communicate what you can and can't offer as a mentor, otherwise you can get sucked into areas beyond your skill-set. Clarity manages customer's expectations and avoids unnecessary confusion."

Positioning is all: whether you are running a restaurant, practising as a doctor or providing any service. Positioning involves declaring what you do and don't provide for customers. Recognising the parameters, people can then choose whether to buy your offering. Here are a variety of positioning statements from people in different professions.

THE LEADERSHIP COURSE LEADER

"Let me explain the goals of the programme. It is about: a) Developing Leadership Skills, b) Building Super Teams. c) Improving Coaching Skills. It is not about: a) Providing Sympathy. b) Practising Therapy. c) Transforming Unmotivated Staff. The next two days will, however, provide techniques you can use for tackling tough issues in your team."

THE ATHLETICS COACH

"My role is to help you excel as an athlete. My philosophy is to build on your strengths. Sometimes I will be tough, however, and tackle areas for improvement. Capitalising on your natural talent, I will offer techniques for winning championships. I am not a substitute parent. My role is not to get you out of bed in the morning or nurse you for 24 hours a day. You must show the will to win by taking care of yourself. Do we have a contract? Take 48 hours to think about it, then give me your reply."

THE HOLISTIC DOCTOR

"My philosophy is to focus on prevention as well as cure. Completing your initial medical check, we will then agree on a programme for keeping yourself healthy, which will include eating, exercise and lifestyle. It is your life, so you will be responsible for making this happen. Certainly I will treat any illnesses, such as headaches, rashes or stomach upsets. My philosophy is to focus on you as a whole person, however, rather than just on the symptom. I prefer to put people in charge of their bodies, rather than become dependent on a doctor. What do you think of this approach?"

Clear contracting is the basis for healthy transactions. Confused contracting leads to painful problems. Mentors in one hotel chain, for example, were 'instructed' to deliver tough messages to poor performers. Three errors were set in train. First: The mentors' position was abused. Second: The mentees lost confidence in the hotel chain. Third: The line managers, who lacked courage to communicate tough messages, were let off the hook. Mentors must set clear parameters with their sponsors. They must agree: a) What they are prepared to do in the role. b) What they are not prepared to do in their role. Clear contracting provides the platform for achieving success.

Mentoring is a niche business. Try tackling the exercise called *Clarity*, overleaf, which invites you to say what you can and can't offer customers. Time to explore the final step before going to market.

CLARITY

Different mentors offer different things to their customers. What can you offer? What can't you offer? Clarity helps you to make clear contracts, both with yourself and with your customers.

CAN: The things I can offer in my role as a mentor are

☞ ....

....

☞ ....

....

☞ ....

....

CAN'T: The things I can't offer in my role as a mentor are

☞ ....

....

☞ ....

....

☞ ....

....

CUSTOMERS

"Do work you love with customers that you like," urges David Maister, the author of *True Professionalism*, who advises accountants, lawyers and solicitors. "Sounds idealistic," people argue. Maister takes the opposite view. Pursuing your calling is, he believes, the only *realistic* way to create an outstanding business. Customers will then pick up on your enthusiasm. You must also, of course, show the benefits of buying your service. Doing work you love is the most likely pathway towards fulfilling your purpose.

"Being good at business development involves nothing more than a sincere interest in clients and their problems, and a willingness to go out and spend time being helpful to them," writes David Maister. "Why spend the majority of that life working on *tolerable* stuff for *acceptable* clients when, with some effort in (for example) client relations, marketing, and selling, you can spend your days working on exciting things for *interesting* people? You will be more successful marketing to clients you like, on issues that interest you, than you will to clients you don't care about, on stuff you can barely tolerate."

Sounds promising: but is it feasible? Providing you deliver the goods, the answer is "Yes." Mastering your trade involves overcoming setbacks and performing at a hundred 'Village Halls', rather than immediately starring at the Carnegie Hall. It also involves targeting niche clients. Try completing the exercise called *My Perfect Customers*, overleaf. Who would be your perfect client? Describe three benefits you can offer such a sponsor. Monday morning is a pleasure when you are encouraging inspiring customers and pursuing your vocation.

MY PERFECT CUSTOMERS

Who would be your perfect customers? Would they be individuals, teams or organisations? How often would they buy your services? Why would they want your mentoring services? Describe your perfect customers and the benefits you could offer these people.

The perfect customers would be:

☞ ....

☞ ....

☞ ....

The three key benefits I would offer these customers would be:

☞ ....

☞ ....

☞ ....

One final exercise. Imagine you are a mentee. Today you are having a 2 hour meeting with your Mentor. What would you like to take place? Describe your wishes in the exercise called *My Ideal Mentoring Session,* overleaf. People who seek your advice may prefer something different, of course, so it is helpful to check-out their vision. You can then aim towards achieving their picture of perfection.

Time to move from theory to action. How to translate the philosophy into principles and then into practice? The following chapter explores one way to assist somebody who is looking to find solutions to challenges.

MY IDEAL
MENTORING SESSION

Put yourself in the role of mentee. Imagine that today you
are having a 2-hour meeting with your mentor. What would
constitute an ideal mentoring session? The following
exercise invites you to clarify your picture of perfection.

My ideal mentoring session
would be one where:

☞ ....
....

☞ ....
....

☞ ....
....

☞ ....
....

☞ ....
....

2

THE PRINCIPLES

OF MENTORING

PAUL: THE IMPATIENT MD

Monday morning, 8.30 am. The telephone rings. You are obviously top of somebody's 'To Do' list this week. Putting down the untouched cup of coffee, you reach for the telephone.

"Good morning," says the voice at the other end. "My name is Paul. Three years ago you ran a strategic workshop for the senior team of our publishing house which produces twelve magazines. One year ago I moved from my position as Marketing Director to take over from the MD."

"Let me get straight to the point," continues Paul. "Right now most of our company is successful, but some magazines are in trouble. Two departments desperately need to change their culture. Incremental changes won't be enough; they need a complete revolution. Can we meet later this week to discuss how to make this happen?"

Scanning your memory, you conjure up a picture of Paul. Fast talking, he was bright and impatient. Quality conscious, he was the only director who stayed behind to clear the coffee cups at the end of the strategy workshop. Collecting your thoughts, you buy time by saying:

"Glad to hear most magazines are successful. I'm sure we can fix a time to meet this week. Can you give me a quick picture of the business? What is going well? What could be better and how? Perhaps we can then decide the topics to discuss in our meeting."

"The business has twelve titles," explains Paul, launching into his view of the company. "They operate in three distinct market sectors: Sports, Lifestyle and Finance. The Sports and Lifestyle magazines are fine. Run by dedicated staff who are highly professional but a bit 'off the wall', they earn good profits. The Finance Sector is the problem child. The three magazines in this market are staffed by people from the 'old school'. Stuck in a time warp, they still write for their 1970's buddies in insurance and banking."

"How on earth have the senior managers survived until

today?" you ask. "From what I recall, you were not the world's best counsellor."

"Guilty m'lud," laughs Paul. "My first months were spent capitalising on the strong parts of the business. Cash is coming in from those magazines, but the Finance Titles are badly haemorrhaging. Tough decision-making is normally right up my street but, in this instance, I'd like to use you as a sounding board. How are you fixed for Thursday?"

Paul is an early morning person, so you agree to meet off-site at 8.00 am in London. You will fix a hotel conference room. Before then you need more information about his agenda, so you say:

"Looking forward to meeting you on Thursday. One request. The more specific the agenda for our time together, the more likely we are to be successful. While you have given me a good picture of the business, can you fax-or e-mail-to me the specific challenges you want to discuss that morning?"

"One thing to bear in mind when doing this: 'What is the real result you want to achieve?' Is it: 'How to revolutionise the culture in the Finance magazines?' Or is it something greater, such as: 'How to build a successful business?' We must focus on the real 'What?', before moving to the 'How?' Knowing the burning issues ahead of time provides the chance to start thinking of possible solutions."

Paul agrees to e-mail his agenda during the next 24 hours. Putting down the phone, you switch on the kettle to brew a fresh cup of coffee. The meeting with Paul promises to be lively, because he does not suffer fools gladly. As in many Mentoring sessions, at this moment you have no idea of the eventual outcome. Picturing the hotel conference room, you mentally rehearse what might happen on Thursday morning.

PREPARING FOR THE SESSION

How to run your meeting with Paul? How to deal with any 'curved ball' questions? How to orchestrate the session so he leaves the room having fulfilled his agenda? Mentoring works well when you are able:

- To get the right balance between 'Pulling' and 'Pushing'.
- To do the Practical and Mental Preparation.
- To follow the 'Five C' Model for running the session.

Let's explore these steps in greater detail.

THE BALANCE BETWEEN PULLING AND PUSHING

Good mentors are like good educators. 'Starting where the person is at', they nurture learning in a discussion by using two main methods: 'Pulling' and 'Pushing'.

- PULLING calls for being able:
  - To offer a sanctuary.
  - To offer a safe place where the person feels able to share their agenda, interests and goals.
  - To offer support by listening, asking the right questions and drawing-out the person's own answers to problems.

- PUSHING calls for being able:
  - To offer stimulation.
  - To offer creative ideas, challenges, knowledge, success stories, models, tools, leading edge thinking and wisdom.
  - To offer 'take home' value that the person finds relevant and rewarding.

Good mentors balance these two approaches. When in doubt, they 'Pull' rather than 'Push'. Why? The mentee must stay in charge and fulfil their agenda. Mentors ensure the mentee finds the session personal, practical and profitable.

THE PRACTICAL AND MENTAL PREPARATION

The practical preparation is simple. It involves booking the hotel room, fixing a flip chart and arranging travel. Must you see the person off-site? Not necessarily, but there are three advantages to meeting away from their office.

- They are more likely to devote quality time, and avoid distractions, if you meet off-site.

- They may feel more comfortable talking about work challenges on 'neutral ground'.

- They must invest time in travelling, which makes the meeting 'special', rather than part of the daily routine. Time spent travelling to the session offers the opportunity to anticipate and prepare mentally. Time spent travelling home provides the chance to reflect on the learning.

How to run the actual session? Entitled 'The Mentor's Road Map', the *shaded pages* throughout this chapter provide trigger questions you can use to help the person to find creative solutions to challenges. Starting with topics you can cover 'Before the Session', these pages provide a series of milestones you can use to keep on track during the meeting.

Good preparation calls for clarifying the goals for the session. Back to Paul, who e-mails the topics he wants to tackle on Thursday. His issues are:

AGENDA

- How to tackle the problems posed by 'old style' senior managers of the three magazines in the Finance Market?

- How to take the next quantum leap towards building a company that has twelve, or more, successful titles in the areas of Sports, Lifestyle and Finance?

- How to educate all my staff to recognise the steps we must take to remain competitive in the future?

THE MENTOR'S ROADMAP

The *shaded sections* in this chapter provide possible questions that you can ask at each stage of the mentoring process. Many questions cover similar ground, so choose those which fit your own style. One key point. Some straddle both personal and professional life. It is important to use the questions you feel comfortable with and that fit the type of mentoring session you are running.

BEFORE THE SESSION:

SOME POSSIBLE QUESTIONS

- What issues would you like to discuss in the session?

- What are the key challenges you face in your work?

- What are the results you would like to achieve?

- What for you would make it a successful session?

- Could you please fax – or e-mail – the key challenges you would like to discuss during the session?

Paul's agenda sounds straightforward, but how to deal with the unexpected? Mental preparation is crucial. Sports psychologists have popularised techniques such as visualisation, for example, to anticipate events and achieve peak performance. Mental rehearsal can also be applied to your meeting with Paul. Starting with the practical issues, you may wish to imagine yourself:

- Getting to the hotel an hour early.

- Setting-up the flip chart and pens.

- Checking with the hotel to make sure coffee and tea will arrive at 8.00.

- Relaxing and sitting in the reception waiting for Paul.

- Seeing him enter through the door and look around the reception.

- Walking across to shake his hand.

- Greeting him in an informal but professional way.

- Sharing some banter about his favourite soccer team, Chelsea.

- Leading the way to the conference room.

- Asking him which chair he prefers.

- Serving him coffee or tea.

- Thanking him for the call, the e-mail and the agenda.

- Making a clear contract about his timetable and the length of the meeting this morning.

- Telling him that you have done some thinking about his challenges and possible solutions.

- Positioning what you can offer in the session. For example: A 'Third Ear'; some possible solutions to the challenges; success stories from other companies that have faced similar issues.

– Positioning what you can't offer.

– Making clear contracts about the expectations and goals for the session.

– Etc.

Mental preparation also calls for engaging in some imaginative pre-work on Paul's challenges. The top topic on his agenda, for example, is: "How to tackle the problems posed by 'old style' senior managers of the three magazines in the Finance Market?" Taking a piece of paper, sketch out your answers to the following questions:

a) What do you see as the choices for tackling the challenge?

b) What do you think *he* will see as the choices for tackling the challenge?

c) What might be some possible creative solutions?

Spontaneity takes a lot of planning. You may therefore wish to imagine going through the 'Five C' Principles. The model provides a road map, not a script, so apply it in your own way. After concluding all the pre-work, it is time to relax and look forward to Thursday. Let's move on to the meeting with Paul.

THE 'FIVE C MODEL' FOR RUNNING THE MENTORING SESSION

Thursday arrives, but sometimes the best laid plans go awry. Returning to the reception area after setting-up the conference room, you see Paul entering the restaurant at 7.45. Greeting him as he is about to sit down, you decide to have breakfast together. His early arrival wasn't in your rehearsal, but it provides time to catch up on the social chat.

Twenty minutes later, moving on to the toast and marmalade, you ask: "Is it okay to talk about your business?" Paul is highly visual. Taking out a blank pad, he sketches his company's organisation chart. Between mouthfuls of coffee, he draws strong arrows pointing to where he sees the problems. "Shall we go to the conference room?" you ask. Paul says he has one telephone call to make and will be with you in five minutes. Picking up the bill for breakfast, you pay the cashier.

STEP ONE: CHALLENGES

"The biggest issue is how to transform the senior managers in the Finance Magazines," explains Paul. "The rest of the business is doing superbly. The mammoth task is how to get these 'old boys' into the 20th Century, never mind the 21st."

"Let's consider all the topics to tackle today," you say, unveiling the list you have earlier written on the flip chart. "Are there any more items you want to add?"

- How to tackle the problems posed by 'old style' senior managers of the three magazines in the Finance Market?

- How to take the next quantum leap in building a company that will have twelve, or more, successful titles in the areas of Sports, Lifestyle and Finance?

- How to educate all my staff to recognise the steps we must take to remain competitive in the future?

"Seems enough to fill the next hour," says Paul. "More issues might come to the surface as we talk during the morning."

Time to make a decision. Two options confront you at this point of the meeting:

a) You can rush in and try to 'prove your worth' by working to 'solve' the first issue.

b) You can ask Paul to give you his picture of where he wants the business to go in the future.

Choosing the second route is often more advisable. Why? Paul's challenges must be seen in the framework of his long-term goals. The three burning issues may also be connected. Seeing these links calls for grasping the big picture. Levelling with Paul, you promise to return to the first topic. Any suggestions you give, however, must fit into the wider context. You ask about his business vision.

"Leap-frogging three years forward: What is your picture of the publishing house? Who will be your main customers? What businesses will you be in: Sports, Lifestyle, Finance? What will be your profitability? What technological changes will have taken place in the market? Where will the company be located? How many staff will be employed on the magazines? What will be their characteristics? Who will remain from the present staff? What other types of staff will you need to hire?"

Paul is a visionary. Arie de Geus, author of *The Living Company*, says such people have 'A Memory of the Future.' Peak performers project themselves into the future to picture what is happening in their chosen field. They then rehearse various strategies for achieving success. Storing the information in their unconscious, they return to the present. Sometimes they act on the information today, other times they wait until the foreseen situation arises, then dip into their unconscious to select the best strategy. Peak performers are proactive. They are able to anticipate and shape the future. Poor performers are reactive. Stumbling from crisis to crisis, they seldom think ahead. They have little realistic 'Memory of the Future'.

"Despite massive technological changes, the principles of successful publishing will remain the same," says Paul, "The Number One priority will be to create superb quality magazines that build customer loyalty."

Customers will become increasingly 'promiscuous'. Surfing the Internet, interactive TV and other media, they will 'pick and mix' to fit their own agenda. What is the answer? Trading in 'the age of the never-satisfied customer' provides opportunities for the brilliant niche supplier. Paul believes it will be vital: a) To publish highly targeted magazines. b) To employ superb people who write exciting material that matches their customers' agendas and aspirations. c) To attract the right advertisers. Street-wise employees will hold the key to success. They must be close to their customers, ready to turn on a sixpence (or a Euro) and hungry to stay ahead of the game.

What about the Financial Titles in his stable? Will they still exist? If not, this immediately solves the problem.

"The whole concept of 'Managing Your Money' will become critical with the withering of Welfare State," explains Paul. "Personal finance will top many people's agendas. How to meet this growing customer demand? Repositioning two of the present financial titles, I will link these to our Lifestyle magazines. One of the present titles will survive. But its target group will be dedicated professionals who work in, for example, Maritime Insurance. Staff remaining at that magazine must learn how to pay their way in the world. The bottom-line is that two of our present financial titles will be repositioned to meet the emerging market for advice on making the most of your money."

"Bearing this picture in mind," you say, "let's return to today's topics. Which is the first challenge you want to tackle?"

"I still want to explore how to change the culture in the Finance Magazines," says Paul. "Talking about the future, however, has set me thinking about different ways to solve the problem."

Mentoring works best when people get an overview of their situation. Tempting as it is to rush into solving the mentee's burning issue, it often helps to see things from the 'helicopter'. The page opposite, headed *Challenges: Some Possible Questions,* offers a framework you can use to get a full picture of the person's goals.

CHALLENGES:
SOME POSSIBLE QUESTIONS

- What are your goals for the session? What issues would you like to discuss? What are the results you would like to achieve? What for you would make it a successful session?

- What are the key challenges you face in your work? What are the key things you need to focus on in the next year? What are the three key things you – or your business – can do to give yourself the greatest chance of success?

- Which is the first challenge you want to explore? Can you give me a picture of what is happening? Can you give me a specific example? What would you like to happen instead? What would be a positive outcome? What are the *real results* you would like to achieve?

- Before exploring this challenge more deeply, let's revisit your own individual contribution to your work. What are your strengths? What do you enjoy doing? What do you do best? What is your picture of perfection? Looking back in future years, what will you have done that will mean that you consider your work – or life – to have been successful?

- Let's go back and explore the first challenge you want to tackle.

STEP TWO: CHOICES

"What do you see as your possible options for tackling the 'old style' senior management?" you ask Paul.

"Changing the culture in the finance magazines is a good starting point," explains Paul, "but now we are looking at something more fundamental. Today's discussion convinces me the whole business must take a quantum leap forward. Starting with the finance magazines, however, I see five or six possibilities."

Moving over to the flip chart, you sketch out Paul's ideas. He outlines the following alternatives:

a) To do nothing.

"This strategy has run its course, now it's time to act," says Paul. "Editors and journalists on these magazines have produced reasonable copy in the past, but it is has been targeted towards specialists in banking and insurance, which is a diminishing market. Procrastinating is no longer an option."

b) To persuade the senior managers to alter their behaviour and bring about culture change.

Not realistic. Strong on technical knowledge, the senior managers are weak on people management. Nine out of ten people revert to their preferred style under pressure, maintains Paul. Better to harness the managers' talents to make a more beneficial contribution to the company.

c) To install a new management team.

Attractive as this option is, key questions must be answered. Where to find the right people? Does he promote from within the finance magazines? Does he transplant a management team from elsewhere within the company? Does he recruit people from outside? Paul prefers to promote from within, but this may cause complications.

d) To run the finance magazines himself.

"Turning around the magazines would give me a buzz," says Paul, "but it's probably not the right thing for the business. Don't kick this option into touch, however, because it might be useful as a fall-back plan."

e) To reposition two of the financial titles, linking them to the Lifestyle magazines and focusing on 'Managing Your Money'.

The exciting option, feels Paul. Revamping the magazines also offers the vehicle for changing the culture. The third title can stay, providing it remains profitable. It's editors must become more commercial, however, selling know-how to professionals in Maritime Insurance.

f) To sell-off or close the magazines.

"A Management Buy-Out funded by the present editors would be right up my street," comments Paul. "Joking aside, it's not a bad idea. Buyers won't be thick on the ground, so we can give our present staff the first shot. Closing the magazines is possible, but I would prefer to sell and gather cash to invest in future projects."

"Can you see any more options for tackling the challenge?" you ask.

"The six you've mapped-out on the flip chart cover all my thinking," replies Paul. "My inclination is to immediately launch into a plan of action. But it will be useful to consider the implications, which will eliminate the non-starters."

Good mentors encourage the person to talk until they have exhausted all potential options. What if you see a road they have failed to highlight? Decide whether it is appropriate to share your view at this stage. If you believe it will be beneficial, give them a clear message. Make a positioning statement and contract by saying something like:

"One or two other routes may be worth considering. Do you

want me to share these now or shall I wait until we explore the creative solutions?"

Mentees are hungry for answers, so they will be happy to hear your suggestions. 'Keep your powder dry,' is the advice, however, so as to balance the 'Pulling' and 'Pushing'. Why? The mentee may still have some distance to go before exploring all their ideas. They must also see the consequences. Ownership is the springboard to setting off in new directions. Checking the person's 'gut feeling' about the road they wish to travel is therefore crucial. Paradox rears its head at this point, because fine 'Pulling Questions' often contain a respectful element of 'Pushing', inviting the mentee to focus on their real life agenda. Good mentors ensure the person has emptied their head – or heart – before presenting anything that might be construed as a possible solution.

The following pages provide tools for achieving this task. *My Possible Options* is an exercise that invites the person to outline their alternatives. Part One is appropriate at this stage. Part Two and Part Three are useful later when exploring the various consequences. *Choices: Some Possible Questions* offers trigger questions for covering similar ground. Time to move on to the next stage.

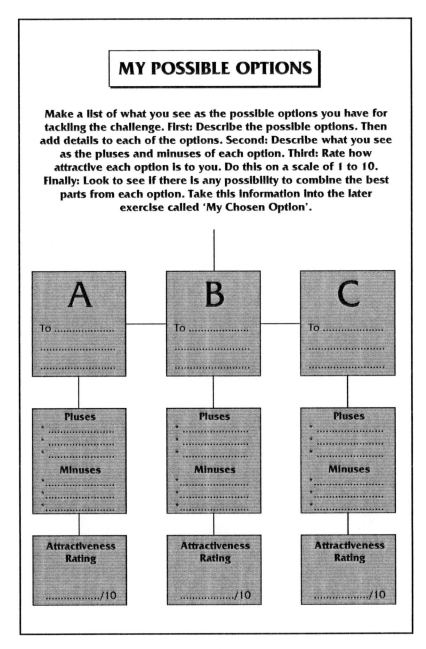

MY POSSIBLE OPTIONS

Make a list of what you see as the possible options you have for tackling the challenge. First: Describe the possible options. Then add details to each of the options. Second: Describe what you see as the pluses and minuses of each option. Third: Rate how attractive each option is to you. Do this on a scale of 1 to 10. Finally: Look to see if there is any possibility to combine the best parts from each option. Take this information into the later exercise called 'My Chosen Option'.

A

To ....
....
....

Pluses
* ....
* ....
* ....

Minuses
* ....
* ....
* ....

Attractiveness Rating

................/10

B

To ....
....
....

Pluses
* ....
* ....
* ....

Minuses
* ....
* ....
* ....

Attractiveness Rating

................/10

C

To ....
....
....

Pluses
* ....
* ....
* ....

Minuses
* ....
* ....
* ....

Attractiveness Rating

................/10

CHOICES:
POSSIBLE QUESTIONS

Looking at the first challenge:

- What do you see as the possible options you have for tackling the challenge?

- What is Option A? Maintaining the status quo and doing nothing is sometimes an option, though maybe not one that is attractive. Is this a possibility in your case? If so: What do you think would happen if you did nothing?

- What do you see as Option B? Can you describe the steps to take if you followed this option? Every option has both pluses and minuses and later on we will be considering these consequences. For the moment, however, let's just explore what you see as all your possible options for tackling this challenge

- What do you see as Option C? Option D? Option E? Can you think of any other possible options? What else have you tried before? What were the consequences? Do you see any of these as possible options? Is there anything we haven't thought of so far? If so, let's add these to the list of possibilities?

- Does that seem enough? If so, let's go on to consider the consequences. We can always come back later and add to the options.

STEP THREE: CONSEQUENCES

Fifteen minutes are devoted to navigating the implications of pursuing each road. Taking the company's point of view, you list the likely pluses and minuses. Leaving Paul to take the lead, you summarise the options on the flip chart.

a) To do nothing.

Pluses: None that are obvious. The only winners will be senior managers who are waiting to pick up their pension.

Minuses: Massive haemorrhaging of money and talent. The market for these financial magazines is diminishing. 'Old style' macho-management will drive away young journalists in tune with today's market.

b) To persuade the senior managers to alter their behaviour to bring about culture change.

Pluses: Provides continuity. Gives another chance to the senior managers. May retain some key people who might otherwise leave the company.

Minuses: Time-consuming. Unlikely to succeed. People seldom change habits, preferring to stick to their skill-sets. Paul, or other change agents, must act as 'cops' to ensure the new behaviour is embedded into the culture.

c) To install a new management team.

Pluses: Fresh blood. Support for the street-wise journalists presently working on the financial magazines. Strong likelihood of being market-driven and boosting profits.

Minuses: Difficult to get the right people. Should we promote from within or kidnap talent? Senior management casualties, leading to internal resentment and poor morale. Paul to spend months ensuring the new team is on track.

d) To run the finance magazines himself.

Pluses: Paul would enjoy the job. Ninety per cent likelihood of launching successful magazines.

Minuses: Casualties. Paul practising remedial treatment on the company's 'problem child', but taking his eye off the total business. Fresh management team must still be found and groomed to take over within one year.

e) To reposition two of the financial titles, linking them to the Lifestyle magazines and focusing on 'Managing Your Money'.

Pluses: The revolution is inevitable. Better to revamp the titles now, rather than later. Repositioning the magazines provides the 'Trojan Horse' for changing the culture. Re-launching two titles will be exciting. Fresh management teams can be put in place and given freedom to fulfil their brief. Current senior managers can be invited to examine their skill-base and show how they want to contribute to the new magazines.

Minuses: Tough to get the right editors and journalists. 'Selling' the idea will meet resistance. Solution: this isn't a 'debate'. The world is moving on, the changes must happen. People can decide whether or not they want to be part of the future business. Casualties will occur. Paul will manage these human factors in a way that people perceive as moral and generous.

f) To sell-off or close the magazines.

Pluses: Gets rid of the problem. Cash injection if sold to an internal or external bidder. Time released to spend on the successful parts of the business.

Minuses: Casualties. Weakening the brand. Failure to capitalise on the emerging market opportunities.

Time to check Paul's gut reaction. Looking at the six alternatives, how appealing does he find each one? On a scale 0-10, he is invited to rate the attractiveness of the different options. It's okay to give the same score to two or more of the routes. Paul takes a minute to contemplate, then scrawls his scores out of 10. Moving over to the flip chart, he explains his verdict.

"Two or three options stand out, the rest are nowhere. Here are my ratings."

- Doing nothing: 0/10

- Persuading the senior managers to change: 3/10

- Installing a new management team: 9/10

- Taking it over myself: 8/10

- Repositioning the finance magazines: 9/10

- Selling for a good price: 6/10

"Looks like it's time to launch the new magazines with a fresh management team," adds Paul. "What do you think?"

"Seems like an exciting venture," you reply. "If you are willing, however, I'd like to go a little deeper into this solution. Then we will move on to your action plan. Is that okay?"

Mentees often cross a Rubicon when they start to feel strongly about pursuing a certain road. The following page offers a framework for achieving this task. *Consequences: Some Questions* provides trigger questions for prompting them to talk through the implications. Rating the attractiveness of each option is a useful guide to setting their inner compass. People are more likely to succeed when implementing a strategy they can 'own' and believe in. So it is vital to follow their flow and preferred direction. Time to move on. Mentors come into their own at the next stage, when they can really earn their corn.

CONSEQUENCES:
SOME POSSIBLE QUESTIONS

- What do you see as the pluses and minuses involved in pursuing Option A? Are there any positives? Choosing the status quo, for example, might not seem attractive. But there may be some benefits, even if they are not immediately obvious. Let's move-on to look at the downside. What do you see as the minuses of taking Option A? Describe all the possible negatives.

- What do you see as the pluses and minuses involved in pursuing Option B? Option C? Option D? Option E? Let's build up a complete picture of the consequences involved in pursuing the different options for tackling this challenge.

- We will soon be moving on towards exploring some potential creative solutions. But first I would like you to check your gut feeling for each of the possibilities you have described.

- Take a look at the different routes you can take: How attractive do you find each of these options? Take a moment to rate the attractiveness of each possible option. Do this on a scale 0 – 10. You might, for example, have two options that are equally appealing and rate both of them as 9/10. On the other hand, several might be horrendous and rate no more than 1 or 2 out of 10. Over to you. Take a minute to rate each of the possible options.

STEP FOUR: CREATIVE SOLUTIONS

"Can we pool our ideas for solving the problem?" you ask. "Can't guarantee any miracles, but is it okay to offer some suggestions?"

"Go ahead, all ideas welcome," responds Paul. "My mind is made up about the future of the financial magazines, but fresh views can be added to the melting pot."

Turning to the flip chart, you flick back to the agenda for the meeting. Paul's burning issues were:

- Changing the culture in the finance magazines.

- Taking a quantum leap forward in the company so that it will have twelve, or more, successful titles in Sports, Lifestyle and Finance.

- Educating staff to recognise the steps the company must take to remain competitive in the future.

Providing the right vehicle is employed, you explain, the publishing house may be able to tackle all three issues simultaneously. Starting from the top, however, you will focus on the first topic: How to change the 'old style' management and inject new life into the finance magazines? Paul stares at the flip chart. Looking thoughtful, he starts scribbling notes on his pad.

"Carry on talking," he says. "My head is bursting with ideas for getting the business to take a quantum leap. Share your suggestions, I am listening."

"Looking at your preferred routes for tackling the first challenge, let's see if there are any possible connections," you say. "The roads you find most attractive are:

- To launch the new magazines.

- To install a new management team.

- To run the magazine yourself.

"What is the best part of each road? Is it possible to combine these parts into a new road?"

"Some parts are now set in stone," Paul answers. "The Personal Finance magazines must be launched and fresh managers hired; that issue is beyond debate. The tough question concerns my own role. Leading the magazines would be exciting, but cramp the new managers' style. My standards are incredibly high, so I am always tempted to interfere. Any suggestions?"

"Managing Directors must install people they trust to lead any new venture," you say. "Otherwise the MD lies in bed at night wondering whether staff are delivering top quality. Who are the 'Trustees' in your business? Trustees embody the spirit of the company. They live the values and deliver high standards. Have you got a Trustee who could head the finance magazines?"

"Denise fits the bill perfectly," replies Paul. "People call her a 'Parachute Packer'. She fulfils her promises and finishes jobs properly. Denise would relish the challenge, but is presently driving another project in the business. I must decide how serious I am about: a) Launching the magazines; b) Leaving the running of the magazines to the new management team. Three years ago I was on the receiving end of a hand-over that went badly wrong."

Paul's explores his transition strategy. Step One will be to approach Denise. Providing she accepts the role, he will give her a crystal clear brief and freedom to pick her own team. Step Two will be for him to meet the incumbent senior managers of the finance magazines. Explaining the repositioning, Paul will pay respect to their specialist knowledge and invite each person to clarify their future contribution to the publishing house. Step Three will be to provide practical support to Denise's team. He must offer them a budget, resources and a profit share. Paul might even offer his services as an internal consultant to the new magazines. Dangerous ground, but he has a nose for the market.

"Denise is meeting me tomorrow," says Paul. "I will outline the new role and ask her to decide over the weekend. My gut tells me this is the right way forward. Ten minutes ago you mentioned the solution of tackling all three goals at once. What do you propose?"

"People work best when they have a shared picture of perfection," you explain. "One possibility is to involve all your 400 staff in an educational workshop that focuses on the future world of magazine publishing. People can explore changes over the next five years in technology, the market and lifestyle. Apart from acting as a 'Trojan Horse' for changing the culture, this event will fulfil the two other goals:

- To get the company to take a quantum leap forward.

- To get all your staff to recognise the steps the company must take to remain competitive in the future.

"Paul, you are a strong-willed visionary; so you must communicate your vision for the magazines. You are reliant on knowledge workers, however, who must take ownership for building up the picture. Otherwise, why should they bother to reach the goal? Staff must then present action plans for ensuring their respective magazines stay ahead of the field. Branding the workshop may be helpful, calling it something like: '20/20 Publishing'."

"My magazines need a revolution: the publishing equivalent of the Fosbery Flop," explains Paul. "The 20/20 notion mirrors some ideas I have had for us taking a giant leap forward. My perennial concern is: 'How can I get my people to see what I see?' I have reservations, however, about transplanting some of the suggestions."

Paul stresses four points about an event such as '20/20 Publishing'. First: The company must run the workshop themselves. Design may call for expert input, but they have in-house people who can perform the delivery. Second: They must create their own branding. '20/20 Publishing' is an old title, so they will invent their own name. Third: They are a media company, so the venture must by backed-up by superb materials, such as workbooks, videos and follow-up newsletters. Fourth: They must produce quick wins. Visible results provide a persuasive argument to sceptical knowledge workers. Paul wants to mull over the idea for a few minutes.

"Time to return to solid ground," he says. "Friday will be a good time to ask Denise if she wants to launch the financial magazines. Crafting a 'Plan B' might also be worth considering, just in case she refuses. Let's get the show on the road."

Mentors employ their personal strengths to explore potential solutions. They may use practical exercises, success stories, creative techniques, lateral thinking or simply listening and talking. What are your preferred methods? *Creative Solutions: Some Questions* provides trigger questions for stimulating the person's imagination. *My Chosen Option* follows on from the earlier exercise inviting them to draw the possible roads they can travel. After settling on their chosen route, it asks the person to start sketching an action plan for pursuing this road. Time to move on to the final stage.

CREATIVE SOLUTIONS
SOME POSSIBLE QUESTIONS

Let's take a helicopter view of your options and see if there are any possible creative solutions:

- Let's start by going back and re-establishing your goals.

    - What are the real results you want to achieve?
    - How can you do your best to achieve these results?
    - When do you want to achieve these results?

- Looking at the different options you have outlined: Is it possible to take the best parts from each option and create a new road? How would this look in practice?

- Let's look back for a moment and learn from your successful history. Have you ever been in a similar situation in the past and managed it successfully? What did you do right? What are your successful patterns in your life and work? How can you follow these paths again in the future?

- Sometimes we can get too close to events. Imagine for a moment that you are an outside consultant who is hired to give tough but fair advice. What advice would you give to yourself to tackle the challenge and reach your goals?

- Let's explore what we can learn from best practice and positive models. Are there any other people, teams or organisations that have successfully managed this kind of challenge? What did they do to manage it successfully? How can we follow these principles in your own way?

- Let's imagine you had a blank piece of paper. What would you do if: a) You could start your organisation again tomorrow? b) You could rebuild your team again tomorrow? c) You could do whatever you needed to fulfil your picture of perfection? What would you do? How can you follow these principles in this situation?

- Let's focus on your best contribution to your corporation. What are your strengths? How can you use these to tackle this challenge? What help do you need from people with other skills?

- Let's focus on your sponsors. Who are your key sponsors? What do they want? How can you satisfy these people? What support do you need from your sponsors? How can you make a clear contract with them and make sure you satisfy your sponsors?

- Let's conclude by exploring any other possibilities. Looking at the challenge: Is there anything else you can do? Are there any 'far out' possibilities? Are there any other imaginative solutions?

- Let's settle on the route you want to pursue. Looking at what we have discussed: What is your chosen option? What must you do to make it happen?

- Finally: What is your back-up plan? What do you want to do if your first option does not succeed? What are your second and third options?

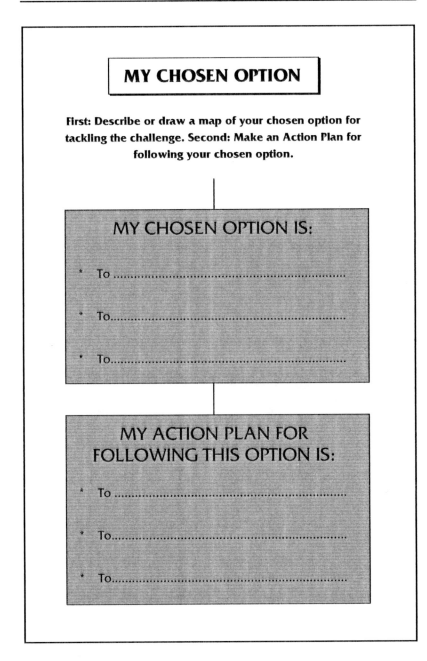

MY CHOSEN OPTION

First: Describe or draw a map of your chosen option for tackling the challenge. Second: Make an Action Plan for following your chosen option.

MY CHOSEN OPTION IS:

* To ....

* To...

* To...

MY ACTION PLAN FOR FOLLOWING THIS OPTION IS:

* To ....

* To...

* To...

STEP FIVE: CONCLUSIONS

"Shall we start with your back-up plan?" you ask. "Imagine the worst-case scenario. If Denise refuses your offer to launch the Personal Finance magazines, what are your other options?"

"Five ideas that I have thought of so far," replies Paul. "My alternatives are:

a) Ask another 'Trustee' to become the editor. Two other people come to mind. Both demonstrate track records of upholding high quality standards.

b) Skip a generation. Two 'Young Turks' want to prove their worth. One disadvantage. Both are younger than the target groups for the magazines. My first goal is to reach the 30-40 age group that must now make key decisions about their financial futures. Good coaching, however, might help the 'Young Turks' to write in a way that reaches this target group.

c) Head-hunt a fresh management team. Costly, but it might be necessary.

d) Run the magazines myself.

e) Give two incumbent senior managers the chance to reposition the financial titles, backed by coaching on a day-to-day basis. Not my chosen option, but still possible if all else fails.

"Enough for Plan B?" jokes Paul. "Given the right freedom and support, I believe Denise will jump at the opportunity."

How long should you devote to the mentee crafting their action plan? Much depends on the person. One MD declared: "I can construct the action plan by myself. I prefer to use my time with you to explore ideas for tackling other challenges." Another MD spent half-an-hour compiling a robust plan that he felt guaranteed success. 'Listening to the customer' and fulfilling their agenda remains the obvious solution. Employ your own judgement on how long to take on translating the vision into visible results.

Paul has been constructing his blueprint throughout the last couple of hours. Tearing three sheets from his note pad, he pushes these across the table. Guiding you through the pages, he explains the following steps for tackling his challenges.

MY ACTION PLAN IS TO:

1) Talk with Denise on Friday about her leading the finance magazines.

   – Make clear contracts about the brief for the magazines, the practical support and the profit share.

   – Give her freedom to pick her own team.

   – Plan how to make a joint announcement about the repositioning of the Personal Finance titles.

   (Implement Plan B if she doesn't want the role.)

2) Arrange one-to-one meetings with the senior managers of the present financial magazines.

   – Communicate the big picture and the repositioning of the financial titles. One magazine will be retained and aimed at professionals in Maritime Insurance.

   – Invite each senior manager to do two things. First: To clarify their strengths. Second: To clarify their best contribution to the company.

   (Speaking in broad terms, I will outline the areas where they may be able to use their talents.)

   – Meet each senior manager again in two weeks time.

     • Agree on their best contribution to the business.
     • Agree on the support they need to do the job.
     • Agree on the targets and make clear contracts.

   What if we must say 'Goodbye'? I will do my best to make sure this is carried out in a way that is moral, fair and generous.

3) Meet my inner-cabinet to discuss involving the 400 staff in a future-oriented workshop, such as '20/20 Publishing'.

 – Ask the inner-cabinet: 'Would it be worthwhile to involve people in anticipating the challenges we face in the next five years?" If so, then:

 – Invite staff from all levels of the company to provide input for the agenda. Ownership is vital, so we would ask people: 'What topics do you believe we should tackle on such a workshop?'

 – Fix provisional dates-perhaps over four days-to involve all 400 people. The workshop will be followed by another one month later. Staff from each magazine will then be expected to present their action plans for tackling the challenges and staying ahead of the field.

"My agenda is finished, at least for this session," says Paul, packing his briefcase. "Sorry about the rush, but I must attend a meeting on the other side of London in an hour. Seriously, it has been helpful. It is always useful to get an outside opinion. Sometimes you get caught up in the day-to-day events, so it is difficult to see things in perspective."

Switching on his mobile phone, Paul walks to the door. His final words are:

"Will call you in a month's time. If I don't, give me a ring to see how I'm progressing. Chelsea are doing well this season, sorry about your soccer team. Thanks again. Will be seeing you."

Time to relax. Surveying the flip charts, coffee cups and note-paper, you reflect on the last three hours. Did you help Paul to land properly? *Conclusions: Some Questions* provides prompts for enabling people to translate their ideas into reality. *The Mentoring Session: My Development* focuses on improving your own efforts, because mentors are only as good as their next performance. Ten minutes later you give yourself permission to come 'Off Duty'. Leaving the conference room, you pay the bill at reception. Time to journey home, time to travel towards the next telephone call.

CONCLUSIONS
SOME POSSIBLE QUESTIONS

- Time to conclude what has emerged from the discussion and how you want to tackle the chosen challenge.

- Let's explore the option you have chosen. What will be the consequences of pursuing this option? What will be the pluses? What will be the minuses? How can you build on the pluses and minimise the minuses? Bearing these consequences in mind: Are you prepared to accept the whole package?

- Let's move on to your action plan. What steps must you take to reach your goals? How can you take these steps? When do you want to begin? What can you do to get some early successes? Make a list of the tasks and timetable.

- Let's conclude with a Reality Check. On a scale 0 – 10:

    a) How much do you rate your desire to pursue this option?

    b) How much do you rate the possibility of it being successful in reaching your goals?

    You can only do your best, of course, and you also have a back-up plan. One final thought: Try to get an early success.

- What is the next challenge you would like to discuss?

THE MENTORING SESSION: MY DEVELOPMENT

Three things I did well in the session

1) ....

2) ....

3) ....

Three things I can do better in the future – and how

1) ....

....

2) ....

....

3) ....

....

3

THE PRACTICE

OF MENTORING

How to work with different kinds of people? The final chapter describes mentoring sessions with a sales-person, a soccer player and the senior team of a small company. It also offers exercises you can use to bring the learning to life.

HELEN: DOING WHAT SHE DOES BEST

Helen was a high flyer in sales. Two years ago, however, she reached a crossroads in her career. Devoted to her clients, she was superb at providing them with user-friendly IT solutions. Far from being a Lone Ranger, she had a track record of running successful project teams. Nobody was surprised when the company suggested that she apply for the role of Sales Director.

"The position is yours," said David, her Managing Director. "providing everything goes well with the interview and psychometric tests."

The tests proved a disaster, so David telephoned me to ask if I could see Helen. The psychologist who conducted them considered her poorly equipped for the role of Sales Director. Clashing with him immediately, she struggled to master the conventional IQ tests. While enjoying the questions about Values, she had problems with those on Critical Thinking. Helen had a history of academic difficulties at school. She compensated for this by teaching herself at home on the computer. A classic deviant who delivers, she travelled 'around the system' to reach her goals.

"The psychologist sent a damning report about her personality style," explained David. "The conclusion was: 'She does not fit the Leadership Template for a Sales Director. Of the 12 factors that contribute to effective leadership, she scores poorly on 8.' Helen isn't the kind of person who fairs well in such tests. Certainly I don't recognise her in what seems to be an 'off the shelf' report. She got poor marks for Team Building, for example, but I have seen her run teams brilliantly."

"Two problems have emerged," continued David. "The first concerns my fellow Directors. Psychometric tests do have some value, but are only part of the picture. Some of my colleagues are getting cold feet, however, and wondering if we should recruit from outside the company. Despite her track record of performing superbly at every level in the business, she must convince them she can be a good Sales Director. The second problem concerns Helen. Her confidence has taken a knock. She needs to regain her joy for work and rediscover her talents. Would you be willing to see her? I positioned this option by saying that I personally talk with you as an outside mentor. She is happy to meet and is expecting a call."

Helen and I met two weeks later. Thirty years old, she was friendly, positive and energetic. She embraced several paradoxes: serious yet humorous, wise yet innocent, strong yet vulnerable. Today's 'Sunrise Professionals' are often highly sophisticated is some areas, but also have wide gaps in their knowledge. Strong-minded yet open, Helen explained that she is willing to improve, even if it meant journeying into unknown territory.

"Apparently I do not fit the 'Leadership Template'," she half-joked. "Academic tests have never suited my style. Turning over the first page of any exam paper drives me into a panic."

People are different, they are not dumb. Helen and I spent twenty minutes discussing the various ways that people learn. Many fight prejudice because they enjoy learning styles different from those rewarded by academia. Jackie Stewart overcame dyslexia to triumph in motor sports and business. Thousands of 11+ 'failures' pursued their own paths towards making significant contributions to the world. Highly visual and feeling, Helen soon recognised her own style for tackling challenges.

a)   She pictured herself performing the challenge successfully.

b)   She experimented with a wide variety of behaviour until she discovered what worked.

c)   She kept doing what worked until she fulfilled her picture.

"The tough part is getting the first picture," explained Helen. "I got confused at school if the teacher told me to solve an algebra problem or do a science experiment. While I was trying to picture the outcome, they kept giving more bits of detailed information. My head felt like exploding, so I gave up. They labelled me 'slow'. Learning on Dad's computer was easier, at least nobody was passing judgement. Now I know my creative style. When selling a business solution to a Senior Management Team, for example, I must first picture myself doing it properly. Accessing the picture is the hard part, the rest is relatively easy."

Discussing learning styles acted as a catharsis. Helen moved on to describe the top three challenges she wanted to tackle. These were:

- To enjoy work again.
- To convince key Senior Managers I can be a good Sales Director.
- To go beyond offering IT solutions and broadening what I can provide for our customers.

Loosely following the Five C Model, I invited her to try several exercises that provided information for tackling her chosen challenges. Helen completed those she felt were relevant and worthwhile. She began by focusing on three issues: a) How to take more charge of her life. b) How to recapture her zest for work. c) How to get back in touch with her talents. The exercises she did were:

✎ SHAPING MY FUTURE

People like to feel in charge of their lives. Some of the greatest fears we have are, for example, being made redundant or suffering a debilitating illness. Viktor Frankl, a survivor of concentration camps, argued that much depends on our attitude. "Man is not free from his conditions," he said, "but he is free to take a stand towards his conditions." This exercise invites you to focus on how much you feel able to shape your future.

1) How much do you feel you can shape your future life? Rate this on the scale 0 – 10. If you feel in charge, you may give a

high score, such as 8 or 9. If you feel that many circumstances are beyond your ability to shape them, you may give a lower score, such as 3 or 4. Mark your rating with an 'A'.

2) How much would you like to feel you can shape your future life? Rate this on the scale 0 – 10. Mark your rating with a 'B'.

3) Turning to the next page, describe:

- The Things I Can Do To Shape My Future.
- The Things I Can't Do To Shape My Future.
- My Action Plan: The Things I Want To Do To Shape My Future.

SHAPING MY FUTURE

A) **How much do you feel you can shape your future life?**

Rate this on the scale 0–10 below.

Mark your rating with an 'A'.

B) **How much would you like to feel you can shape your life?**

Rate this on the scale 0–10 below.

Mark your rating with an 'B'.

| 0 | 1 | 2 | 3 | 4 | 5 | 6 | 7 | 8 | 9 | 10 |

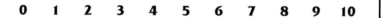

SHAPING MY FUTURE
MY ACTION PLAN

The things I can do to shape my future are:

1)   I can..

2)   I can..

3)   I can..

The things I can't do to shape my future are:

1)   I can't..

2)   I can't..

3)   I can't..

The things I want to do to shape my future are:

1)   I want to...

2)   I want to...

3)   I want to...

✎ *MY TURBO-POWER*

"Some people are Turbo-Powered. Some people are Trabant-Powered," said one M.D. "Some people I can rely on to produce results quickly. Some people I have to chase for months." This exercise invites you to do three things.

1) Describe the times in your work when you are Turbo-Powered. For example: Turning around proposals, fixing computer problems or delivering superb customer service.

2) Describe the times in your work when you are Trabant-Powered. For example: Doing paperwork or attending boring meetings.

3) Describe the things you can do to be more Turbo-Powered in the future. You may also wish to find ways to compensate for-or to avoid-the situations where you are Trabant-Powered.

MY TURBO-POWER

Turbo-power

The times in my work when I am turbo-powered are:

☛ When I...

☛ When I...

☛ When I...

Trabant-power

The times in my work when I am trabant-powered are:

☛ When I...

☛ When I...

☛ When I...

Future turbo-power

The things I can do to be more turbo-powered in the future are:

☛ I can...

☛ I can...

☛ I can...

✎ MY HELICOPTERING

Peak performers balance contradictions when performing at their best. They may, for example, be Visionary and Practical; Focused and Flexible; Serious and Playful. People function best in certain 'elements'. How to find where you perform superbly? One way is to identify situations where you are simultaneously 'Hands-On' and 'Helicoptering'. Great teachers, for instance, are totally involved when lecturing to their students. At the same time, however, they see everything that is happening in the room by 'Helicoptering' over the class. Great soccer players control the ball at their feet yet simultaneously picture where every other player is on the field. This exercise invites you.

1) To identify a situation where you simultaneously experience being 'Hands-On' and 'Helicoptering'.

2) To identify what you do right to perform at your best in this situation.

3) To identify the concrete things you can do to develop these abilities.

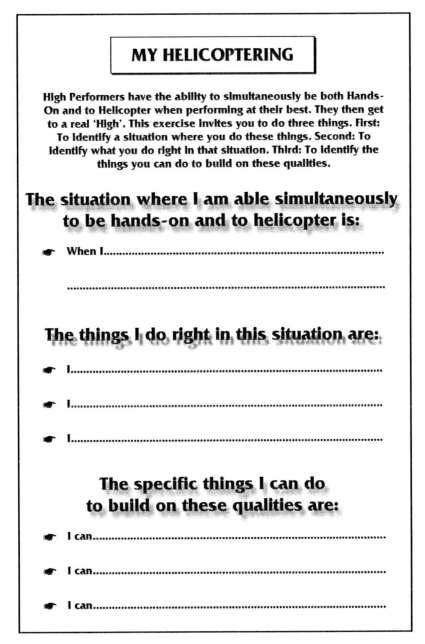

MY HELICOPTERING

High Performers have the ability to simultaneously be both Hands-On and to Helicopter when performing at their best. They then get to a real 'High'. This exercise invites you to do three things. First: To identify a situation where you do these things. Second: To identify what you do right in that situation. Third: To identify the things you can do to build on these qualities.

The situation where I am able simultaneously to be hands-on and to helicopter is:

☞ When I...

....

The things I do right in this situation are:

☞ I...

☞ I...

☞ I...

The specific things I can do to build on these qualities are:

☞ I can...

☞ I can...

☞ I can...

"Shaping the future isn't a problem, so I gave myself 9 out of 10." declared Helen. "Being a survivor, I always land on my feet. Life balance is tougher. My work is more rewarding than my relationships at the moment, but that is down to me. What you give is what you get."

Helen planned to devote more time to 'treating herself' during the next year. She aimed to join a health club, learn judo and continue teaching dyslexic kids. Apart from harnessing her computer skills, this helped her to meet interesting people. She felt able to shape a fulfilling future.

When did she feel Turbo-Powered? An Adrenalin-Driven person, Helen loved the thrill of delivering just before a deadline. Three factors made the effort worthwhile. First: She must believe-in the task. Second: She must stretch herself just beyond her present capabilities. Third: She must deliver to customers, or an internal sponsor, whom she respected. Helen felt turned-on when providing business solutions for her favourite customers. But this posed the question: How to get the right balance between being creative and commercial? She must focus on 'Turbo-Power' activities that benefited the company.

"The 'Helicoptering Exercise' explained a lot," said Helen. "There are three situations where I feel totally involved and also have an overview.

- When making a sales presentation to customers.
- When leading a team of motivated people.
- When dealing with a crisis.

"Sales presentations are where I feel most comfortable," she said "But I see my role as helping customers to get what they want, not as selling."

"Deadlines motivate me. My ritual is to go home and put on some music. I then write the actual words I want my customers to be saying at the end of the presentation. For example: 'I see how the package will boost our bottom-line results. The solution is one that we can customise to fit our needs. This approach has an implementation plan with milestones that we can measure.'"

"Putting the presentation together comes next. Compiling the computer graphics, I write the key points to make with each picture. Starting from their point of view, I consider what each decision-maker wants from our package. Highlighting the benefits, I brainstorm potential difficult questions and list my answers. Combining all these pieces of the jigsaw, I create a picture of people leaving the room looking satisfied. Excited but nervous, I feel ready to make the presentation."

'Starting with the end in mind,' is a well-known technique. But what if a key decision-maker asks a curved ball question? "I become very calm, almost cold," replied Helen. "Everything then goes in slow-motion." The emotion drained away. Hovering above the situation, she became aware of the people, the sounds and everything happening in the room. Helen pictured the different strategies for moving towards her goal. Dipping into her preparation, she chose the appropriate answer to the question. She never got into arguments. "Because then you are dead," she said. Like many knowledge workers who sell, she redefined her work as education. Helen followed the LEAD Model for presenting to customers. This is:

L isten to what the customer wants.

E ducate the customer about the different routes they can take toward getting what they want.

A gree on the route the customer wants to take toward getting what they want.

D eliver what the customer wants.

Staying above the fray, Helen offered her customers a map of the different routes they could take towards achieving the business solution. She continued:

"Sometimes I become detached, as if I do not care whether or not we get the contract. Two of the biggest deals we landed in the last year resulted from telling the client not to buy from us.

Both times key managers in the group asked tough questions. Both times I genuinely put what the client wanted before what I, or my company, wanted. Both times we won bigger contracts than we pitched for in the first place."

Time was pressing, but two things stood out. Helen felt most at home helping her customers to find solutions. She also loved working with motivated people. Both factors had implications for her desire to become Sales Director. Acknowledging these points, I suggested we move on to the second challenge she wanted to consider: "How to convince the key Senior Managers that I can be a good Sales Director.' Helen needed the okay from both her present and potential Sponsors. She tackled the following exercise for clarifying her strategy for achieving this goal.

✎ MY SPONSORS

Sponsors are people you must satisfy in order to thrive in your job. This exercise invites you to do three things:

1) Write the names of each of your Sponsors.

   Some may be people you report to directly. For example: your Manager, your MD and your Customers. Some may be people whose goodwill you depend on to continue in your job. For example: Other Departmental Heads, Key People In The Company, etc. This exercise provides space for only one Sponsor. You may find it useful, however, to continue your list of Sponsors on another piece of paper.

2) Write what you believe each of these Sponsors wants.

   Some Sponsors may only want you to deliver bottom-line results. Other Sponsors may want other things. Much depends on their individual personality styles. One person may prefer to be presented with solutions, rather than problems. A second may like to be given the big picture, rather than the details. A third may want to be fully involved in decisions, rather than hearing them by default. 'Managing Upwards' calls for seeing the world from each Sponsor's point of view.

3) Write what you can do to satisfy each of these Sponsors.

Keeping your integrity and playing to your strengths is crucial. Bearing in mind what you are prepared to offer: What can you do to satisfy each of these Sponsors? The next steps are:

a) To make clear contracts with your Sponsors about the results to achieve.

b) To agree on the support you need to do the job.

c) To deliver the results and fulfil your agreed contract.

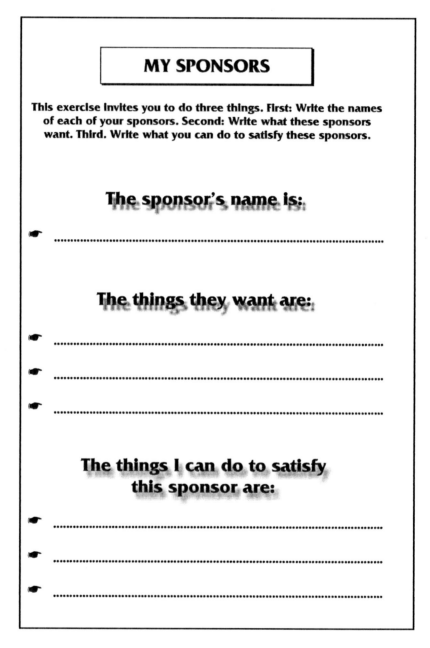

MY SPONSORS

This exercise invites you to do three things. First: Write the names of each of your sponsors. Second: Write what these sponsors want. Third. Write what you can do to satisfy these sponsors.

The sponsor's name is:

☞ ....

The things they want are:

☞ ....

☞ ....

☞ ....

The things I can do to satisfy this sponsor are:

☞ ....

☞ ....

☞ ....

Helen spent half-an-hour listing the Sponsors she must win to become Sales Director. David, the MD, wanted bottom-line results. Talking with him called for giving headlines, rather than social chat. He wanted to be kept informed and hated nasty surprises. The HR Director wanted a boost in staff morale. She also liked people to be given ownership in setting their departmental goals. The Operations Director wanted milestones and measures built into implementation plans. He also liked reports, expense forms and administrative tasks to be completed on time. Helen felt able to present her case in a way that won the Directors' confidence, but she now raised a more fundamental issue. Did she really want to be the Sales Director?

"My concern is whether I can be true to myself and still fit the Leadership Profile," explained Helen. "Today's exercises have confirmed the activities that give me a buzz. My history is to go my own way, rather than fit the mould. I want to continue doing what I love, which means redefining the role of Sales Director. Do you believe this is possible?"

"The Board may buy into your picture of the Sales Director, but only if they see how it will benefit the business," I replied. "Positioning is all. Show how building the job around your strengths will be best for the company, not just for yourself. Reservations may still persist, however, so demonstrate how you will compensate for any perceived weaknesses. Let's begin by defining your own style of leadership."

Great leaders adopt different styles for inspiring people to achieve success. Many focus, however, on values, vision and visible results. Step One is to coalesce people around certain values. Step Two is to encourage them to achieve an inspiring vision. Step Three is to educate and equip people to achieve visible results. Leaders also operate in different fields. They may devote themselves to, for example, Business Leadership, Military Leadership, Creative Leadership, Thought Leadership or another pioneering venture. Great leaders also leave a lasting legacy, they empower people to achieve ongoing success.

Mentors help people to find the best way to express their natural talents. Helen tackled the following exercise to define her approach to the role of Sales Director.

✎ MY PREFERRED LEADERSHIP STYLE

Being true to yourself is one of the foundations for leadership. Building on this base, you can then decide which skills you can add to your professional repertoire. This five-part exercise invites you to clarify your own style of leadership. Describe:

1) The Things I Do Like To Do As A Leader.

   What aspects do you like best? You may enjoy, for example: working with motivated people; involving them in shaping the vision; giving them support to implement the strategy; and guiding them toward achieving success.

2) The Ways I Can Do More Of These Things.

   How can you build on these aspects? You may want to hire motivated people; integrate their views into the vision; hold monthly meetings to ensure they follow the strategy; and use different media to communicate the successes.

3) The Things I Don't Like To Do As A Leader.

   What aspects do you find limiting? You may hate doing administration; sitting in irrelevant meetings; being a 'Nanny' fixing holidays and timetables; and working with unmotivated people.

4) The Ways I Can Compensate For – Or Find Other Ways To Manage – These Things.

   How can you deal with the aspects you find distasteful? Getting a good Operations Manager will be crucial, otherwise you will spend most of your time tied down in the office. There may be no way, however, that you plan to act as a cheerleader for problem people who don't want to be in the team.

5) My Plan For Developing My Leadership Style.

How to improve your style of leadership? You may want to visit customers to clarify their future needs; share this information with your people; gather their input into the vision; agree clear contracts with each person about their contribution; hold monthly meetings to ensure everything is on track; hire an Operations Manager to handle the daily chores; and introduce a weekly newsletter that reports successes. Describe the steps you can take towards developing your natural leadership style.

MY PREFERRED LEADERSHIP STYLE

The things I like to do as leader are:

☞ ....

☞ ....

☞ ....

☞ ....

The ways I can do more of these things are:

☞ ....

☞ ....

☞ ....

☞ ....

The things I don't like to do as leader are:

☛ ....

☛ ....

☛ ....

The ways I can compensate for – or find other ways to manage – these things are:

☛ ....

☛ ....

☛ ....

My plan for developing my leadership style – and also making sure the other things get done – is:

☛ ....
....

☛ ....
....

☛ ....
....

"Recognising the time-consuming activities involved, the Sales Director's role is becoming less attractive," said Helen, "but I'm beginning to see another option. I could start a new business venture alongside our core offerings."

"Customers are asking us to provide Total Solutions, not just IT solutions. David may have a different opinion, but I believe we can offer something special to the market. The USP could be around developing 'Positive Attitudes Towards Technology'. Two Call Centres, for example, have already asked me to involve their front line people in shaping what they want from the next generation of technology. The bottom line is that these contracts will earn us £500k."

"Several 'Red Threads' run through the exercises we have done today," continued Helen. "I like leading motivated people, working directly with customers and exploring new territory. Why not play to my strengths? The fresh business would focus on inspiring people to want to use new technology. My first target would be to win five contracts. Bringing in £750K, for example, would provide the leverage required for adding a second person to the team. We could then expand to fill the market niche. Starting a fresh business is right up my street. Sitting alongside our present core offerings, the new venture would also boost the company's profits. What do you think?"

"Seems like your mind is already made up," I replied. "The challenge is to sell it to your Sponsors. Before moving on to your action plan, however, I would like you to tackle one final exercise that I ask Senior Managers to do every year."

Bright people are an asset to any company. Such people can be hard to manage, however, because their agendas change. Today's turn-on can become tomorrow's turn-off. How to channel their talents? Clear contracting is vital. Employees have a moral obligation to contribute to the company that helps to pay their mortgage. Employers have a moral obligation to make the best use of their people's strengths. How to make this happen? The following exercise is valuable when contracting with knowledge workers. Once agreements are made, it is vital for all people to fulfil their commitments.

✎ MY BEST CONTRIBUTION TO MY COMPANY

Everybody has strengths. The challenge is to channel these talents to create a 'Win-Win' for yourself and your employer. This exercise invites you to clarify how to match your own and your employer's agendas. Describe the following things:

• My Strengths

   What do you do best? When do you 'Helicopter'? When do you experience the 'Tingle Factor'? Describe your top three talents.

• My Best Contribution To My Company.

   What do you believe is the best way to use your talents? Bear in mind that pursuing this route must also bring rewards for the company.

• The Pluses Of Making This Contribution.

   What would be the benefits? Consider these rewards from the point of view of yourself, your customers and your company. Describe the pluses of making your suggested contribution.

• The Minuses Of Making This Contribution.

   What would be the drawbacks? Consider these negatives from the point of view of yourself, your customers and your company. Describe the minuses of making your suggested contribution.

• My Action Plan For Taking Concrete Steps Towards Making My Best Contribution To The Company.

   How to win the key Sponsors? How to emphasise the pluses and manage the minuses? How to get some quick wins? Describe the practical steps you can take to make the best use of your talents.

91

MY BEST CONTRIBUTION TO MY COMPANY

My strengths are:

☞ ....

☞ ....

☞ ....

☞ ....

My best contribution to the Company would be:

☞ ....

☞ ....

☞ ....

☞ ....

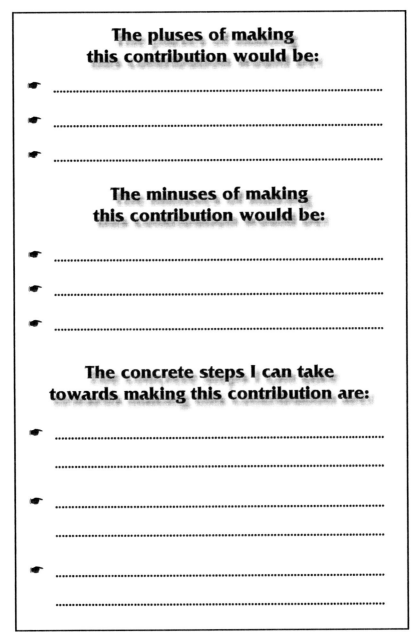

**The pluses of making
this contribution would be:**

☞ ....

☞ ....

☞ ....

**The minuses of making
this contribution would be:**

☞ ....

☞ ....

☞ ....

**The concrete steps I can take
towards making this contribution are:**

☞ ....
....

☞ ....
....

☞ ....
....

Helen spent fifteen minutes doing the exercise. Returning with a mischievous look on her face, she proclaimed.

"I've got a name for the new business. Why not call it PATENT? Positive Attitudes Towards Employing New Technology. Seriously, there is a market for inspiring people to want to use new IT. Taking this step will make an impact on the bottom-line. Money is now squandered by technicians who implement systems without first consulting the people who must use them in their daily work. Winning people's hearts, we can tap the know-how they have in their heads and put the right technology in their hands."

How to translate her dream into reality? Helen's top priority over the next three months was to deliver her previously agreed sales targets. Failure to do so would put the whole budget in jeopardy. Longer term, however, Helen felt there were better ways to channel her talents. She wrote:

My Best Contribution To The Company Would Be To:

- Find and groom somebody to take over my present selling role and bring in £500k a year.

- Get five customers for the new business and win orders to the value of £750k.

- Build and lead a dedicated team which, alongside our core offerings, provides total solutions to customers. Three years down the line this new business should be generating £2 million.

"There is the world of ideas and the world of practice," wrote Matthew Arnold. Forever the practitioner, Helen outlined her action plan.

STEP ONE: TALK WITH DAVID

David's personality style demanded headlines and bottom-line results. Helen must show how making this contribution would benefit the business. The street-wise approach would be to go to him with her first three customers. Providing David gave his backing, she could proceed to the next stage.

STEP TWO: WIN THE KEY SPONSORS

How to tackle this challenge? Helen planned to talk with each Sponsor individually before presenting to them as a Board. Apart from selling the benefits, she must ally any fears. The Directors did not like surprises and had different ways of judging a project. Some liked new ventures; some liked set milestones and specific measures; some just liked to be left in peace. Helen aimed to anticipate and, as far as possible, to satisfy the agenda of each Sponsor.

STEP THREE: GET THE FIRST FIVE CUSTOMERS

Two Call Centres had committed to contracts that would earn £500k. Helen must get one more before approaching David. She listed five potential buyers to call tomorrow. Like mountaineers who imagine themselves descending after reaching the summit of Everest, she visualised going beyond her original goal. She aimed to win ten customers in the first year.

"Looking back," concluded Helen, "the psychologist did me a favour by saying that I don't fit the Leadership Template. Shaping the future has been a lifelong habit and I've always rebounded from knocks. I am looking forward towards running the new business."

Three hours had passed since we started the session. Turning back to the original agenda, we concluded it was time to finish.

"Good luck with the presentation to the Board," I said.

"No problem," answered Helen, "I will start by picturing the actual words I want them to be saying when they leave the room. Thank you for listening. I will ring you when I have my first five customers."

LEROY: TO BE OR NOT TO BE– A GREAT SOCCER PLAYER

Leroy faced a decision. Did he or didn't he want to be a professional athlete? "Awesomely gifted, but impossible to manage," was how coaches described his talents. He was renowned for spectacular antics on and off the field. Bursting onto the soccer scene three years ago, he dribbled past four defenders, rounded the goalkeeper and back-heeled the ball into the net. *Match of The Day* experts drooled over his skills and the world seemed at his feet. Winning a lucrative boot contract meant Leroy would never go hungry. He responded by regularly missing training, preferring to do his sweating dancing at night clubs.

One year later Leroy hit the buffers. Fashionable friends and frequent 'benders' transferred him to the front pages of tabloid newspapers. Poor fitness and rudeness to supporters alienated his team-mates, while crashing his red Ferrari resulted in drink driving charges. Failure to score goals led to him being dropped. Leroy was staring failure in the face at the age of 24. Recommended to seek help by his club captain, who had conquered alcohol problems, we met for an exploratory session. Overcoming some initial wariness, he described losing his goal-scoring touch.

"I have lost my nerve," explained Leroy. "Goal-scoring is something I have found easy ever since I was a kid. Dribbling past defenders, I used to look up and see the goal. Then I just passed the ball into the net. Now I look up and see the massive goalkeeper. Panicking, I take too many touches, then lose the ball. Crowds get on my back and I hide for the rest of the match."

"My manager has given me an ultimatum," Leroy continued. "'Get your act together or get out of the club.' He says I must become a better team player and score 20 'simple' goals each season. My manager thinks I am hooked on scoring spectacular goals. Quoting an old soccer saying, he said: 'You can choose to be a great goal-scorer or a scorer of great goals.' My club captain now goes to Alcoholics Anonymous. He told me: 'It's all about choices. You have to take responsibility for your life, not just for your soccer.' I want to get myself sorted, otherwise I will end up like my Ferrari, lying on the scrap-heap."

THE DESIRE

Great athletes deliver. They have the desire and the discipline required to reach their chosen destination. Did he possess these qualities? Leroy spent 30 minutes mapping-out the roads he could pursue during the next ten years. The next step would be to see if he was prepared to pay the price. Four possibilities emerged. He could choose:

a) To continue with his present life style.

Not so crazy as it sounds. Leroy could still mix with hangers-on and go night-clubbing to get his Adrenalin highs. What about his soccer career? Desperate teams would queue up to take a gamble. Pressured by vocal fans, they would pay several million pounds hoping Leroy would score goals. Britain had three or four clubs that had fallen on hard times. They would pay over the odds to appease supporters. "Why not go abroad?" asked his agent. "I can compile a video of your best goals and send it to clubs on the continent."

The downside? Burned-out at the age of 28. Nomads have no fixed home, which meant little time to see his son, who now lived with his estranged wife. Wasting his talent and disappointing his parents did not appeal to Leroy. He moved on to his next option.

b) To maintain some parts of his life-style while playing soccer at a lower level.

"I'm not disciplined enough to strike the right balance," said Leroy. "How would I spend the afternoons? I'd be tempted to drink with friends or bet on the horses, rather than return for an extra stint on the training field. Besides, I don't want to drop down to play in the Second or Third Division."

The upside? Living some of the 'good life', staying in touch with friends and still playing soccer. The downside? Too many distractions, a shortened career and playing in front of 1,000 people on a cold winter night. "Forget it," said Leroy. Time to move on to his next option.

c) To fully commit himself to being a professional soccer player.

The upside? "Respecting myself and playing soccer at the highest level," said Leroy. "I want to give it my best shot, but it means a dramatic change in lifestyle. My club captain says he will never stop being an alcoholic. He takes 'one day at a time' and the same rule applies to me. Sticking to the new discipline will be tough, but not as painful as losing my soccer. As they say in the game, 'You're a long time retired.' Providing I do the business on the field, the money will take care of itself, but there is more at stake."

"My parents sacrificed a lot in the early years. Disappointing them hurts, but most of all I have let myself down. I used to scoff when team-mates called an older player 'a good pro.' These were unsung heroes who trained hard, battled against injury and put in 30 solid performances every season. Now I want to be 'a good pro.' It's my only chance to play every week, score goals and take part in the World Cup."

The downside? Sweat; hard work; new disciplines; saying 'No' to hangers-on; filling empty afternoons; coping with depression without drink, drugs or fast driving. Leroy looked at his final option.

d) To give up soccer.

"Out of the question," he said. "Looking into the future, two images flash through my head. One is of a successful international player coaching teenagers. The other is of a washed-up, overweight former player telling stories to drunks in bars. Right now I am committing suicide. I want to recapture the feeling I had as a kid, when I lived for nothing else but enjoying soccer."

How to paint a picture of his destination? Leroy needed a vision to hold in his head, especially when times got tough. What were his goals as a professional soccer player? How did he want to be remembered as a person? He tackled the following exercise that focused on his legacy. After completing the exercise, he transferred these goals to a piece of paper and put them in his wallet.

✎ SUCCESS

What do you want to achieve in your life and work? Everybody wants to be happy, but people follow different routes towards finding fulfilment. One person may travel around the world, raise a family and run their own business. Another person may teach children, write a book and pass-on their knowledge. People have different pictures of success.

Imagine that you are looking back in later years. Describe what you will have done that means you have led a fulfilling life. Start with the words: "I will consider my life has been successful if:................." You may want to share your ideas with your partner, a friend or another trusted person. What is your picture of success?

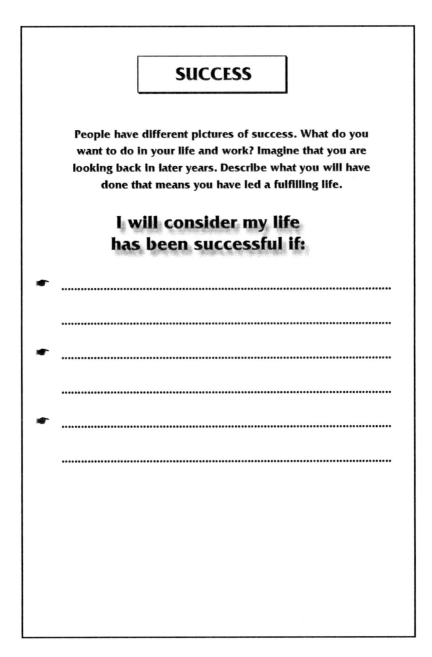

SUCCESS

People have different pictures of success. What do you
want to do in your life and work? Imagine that you are
looking back in later years. Describe what you will have
done that means you have led a fulfilling life.

I will consider my life
has been successful if:

☞ ....

....

☞ ....

....

☞ ....

....

"Life seems simple when you're writing lists on paper, but it isn't that easy," said Leroy. "As we say in the game, 'No team won anything by looking good on paper.' Winning calls for having committed players who train hard, give 100% and perform on the pitch. The same is true when it comes to getting up in the morning and battling through the day. My goals are:

I will consider my life has been successful if:

- I have been a good father to my son.

- I have played over 300 games as a professional soccer player.

- I have played over 30 international matches.

- I have scored over 100 goals.

- I have lived a good life, been a credit to my parents and helped people less fortunate than myself.

"My club captain has changed character completely over the last two years," added Leroy. "Despite having long-term goals, he says it's better to focus on doing your best every moment. He follows this rule whether he is spending time with his kids, playing in a match or giving interviews to the press. Any prizes you win along the way are a bonus. Maybe I need to adopt a similar attitude towards achieving my view of success."

Time to give a rating. On a scale 0-10, how great was Leroy's desire to reach his goals? No question: 10/10. Everybody has dreams, but are they prepared to sweat?

THE DISCIPLINE

"Success has come easily for me in my life," explained Leroy. "Naturally good at ball games, I was always Number 1 in the team. Playing at school and county level, I was the star forward, which meant I never had to fight for my place. Youth team soccer was harder, but my knack for scoring goals meant I could get away with murder. Talented kids have this problem. They are so gifted that they can get by without sweating. Suddenly I am no longer Number 1. My place in the pecking order is Number 16."

Would he fight to be the first choice striker? Gifted young stars frequently throw in the towel when confronted by the narrowing Pyramid. They prefer to sit in pubs, brag to their mates and tell stories about 'what might have been.' Sports players must demonstrate the 'Will' as well as the 'Skill'. Leroy felt committed, but would his resolve stand the test of time? Setbacks could be overcome providing he did two things. First: He must see the benefits to be gained from the sweat. Second: He must find and follow his successful patterns. Let's explore these topics.

Leroy is someone who is Adrenalin-Driven. Such people are addicted to adrenalin, adventure and achievement. Pulling off a massive sales deal, performing rock music or stealing cars, for example, feels exhilarating. They love living life on the edge. Hooked on excitement, they enjoy the highs. "I have to keep getting a bigger hit," said one advertising executive. People can choose healthy or unhealthy ways to get their Adrenalin fixes. Getting a buzz and seeing the benefits from his new approach was essential for Leroy, otherwise he might revert to his old lifestyle.

"The greatest carrot is having a successful career as a professional soccer player," he said. "Some days may be dark, but not as dark as when I sat drinking in the afternoons with my mates in clubs. I now feel strong enough to cope with reality."

Leroy already had the answers within him; the key lay in tapping the healthy side of his character. Everybody has a positive history. Everybody has within them the seeds of success. Everybody has the knowledge of how to overcome setbacks. People can access the healthy patterns that have worked for them in the past, even if this is only 10% of their total life experience. Recognising their own knowledge base, they become hungry to learn from eternal wisdom and leading edge thinking. An outside helper-be it a 'Third Ear', 'Helicopter View' or whatever-can also help them to chart the journey. Many exercises that people find enriching are based on the following framework.

a) People can learn from their own history of success.

b) People can be helped to find their successful patterns.

c) People can follow these patterns and, by applying the relevant wisdom, they can achieve success in the future.

How did this relate to Leroy? Exploring both his past and future, he was invited to select from six exercises that focused on his personal and professional life. Translating the principles into practice would form the basis for following new daily disciplines.

✎ MY FOCUSING EXPERIENCE

People perform remarkable feats when they harness all their powers. Describe a time in your life when you really focused. You may, for example, have studied night and day to pass an exam, conquered tiredness to complete a marathon or put everything else aside to finish a particular project. Looking back at that experience: What did you did right on that occasion? Describe how you can follow these principles to make full use of your powers again in the future.

MY FOCUSING EXPERIENCE

A)   Describe a time in your life when you really focused. This can be in your personal or professional life.

I really focused when...

....

B)   Describe the things you did right to ensure you focused.

I ....

I ....

I ....

C)   Describe how you can follow these paths again in the future. Try to be as specific as possible.

I can..

I can..

I can..

✎ MY BEST TEAM PERFORMANCE

People have different creative styles. Some prefer to work alone, some prefer to work in teams. Even if you like to work by yourself, it is helpful to know how to co-operate with other people. When did you work best in a team?

Leroy chose an away match when his fellow striker was sent off for arguing with the referee. Playing as the one remaining forward, he ran unselfishly and shouted words of encouragement to his colleagues. He finally won a penalty when tripped by the goalkeeper. The spot kick was converted and his team gained a creditable draw. Leroy showed a work ethic in that match that few people thought he possessed. Similar qualities must be demonstrated every week to ensure he played regular top class soccer.

Returning to your own best team performance: What did you do right on that occasion? How can you follow these paths again to make the best use of your talents in a team?

MY BEST TEAM PERFORMANCE

The time I produced my best team performance was:

☞ When I...

The things I did right then to do my best for my team were:

☞ I ....

☞ I ....

☞ I ....

The things I can do to follow these principles to do my best for a team in the future are:

☞ I can...

☞ I can...

☞ I can...

✎ *MY ADRENALIN HIGHS*

When do you feel exhilarated? You may get an adrenalin rush from, for example, closing a sale, climbing rocks, riding horses, performing music, solving a maths problem or whatever. This exercise is in two parts.

1) Describe the times when you get your adrenalin highs.

    Kay, a powerful business consultant, wrote: "When I am speaking to a large audience, playing the lead role in a theatre production and driving fast cars." Try to be as specific as possible when listing the activities that you find exciting.

2) Describe the specific steps you can take to do more of these things and get more adrenalin highs.

    Go for quality, rather than quantity. Kay wrote: "I will take up an offer from a speaker's bureau to act as my agent for booking more big speeches. I will also play one major lead role in our theatre each year. The fast cars will have to be confined to early Sunday morning driving on the M40." Describe the steps you can take to get more feelings of exhilaration.

MY ADRENALIN HIGHS

The times when I get my adrenalin highs are:

1) When I...
....

2) When I...
....

3) When I...
....

The specific steps I can take to do more of these things are:

1) I can...
....

2) I can...
....

3) I can...
....

✎ MY ALARM BELL EXPERIENCES

Such events are 'Wake-Up Calls' that show something is not right in our lives. They can take many different forms, such as: an illness, a car accident, losing a client, feelings of unease or other symptoms. This exercise is in three parts.

1) Describe an 'Alarm Bell' experience you have had in your life. The more recently such an event occurred, the more relevant it is to your present situation.

2) Describe what you learned from this experience.

3) Describe the specific things you can do to apply these lessons in the future.

Healthy people are open to such messages, rather than ignore the warnings or dull the pain. Alarm Bell experiences are a wake-up call summoning people to re-take charge of their lives.

MY ALARM BELL EXPERIENCES

An alarm bell experience I had was:

☞ When I..

....

....

The things I learned from that alarm bell experience were:

☞ ....

☞ ....

☞ ....

The specific ways I can apply these lessons in the future are:

☞ I can..

☞ I can..

☞ I can..

✎ MY BIGGEST CHALLENGE

Muhammad Ali said after losing a world title fight: "Everybody has disappointments in life. Greatness is shown by recovering from those disappointments." Everybody has a history of overcoming setbacks. They may, for example, have recovered from an illness, moved on from a debilitating job or learned to live life again after losing a loved one. This exercise is in three parts.

1) Describe the biggest challenge you have overcome in your life.

2) Describe what you did right to overcome that challenge.

3) Describe how you can follow these principles to overcome challenges in the future.

People can tap their inner strength by finding and following their patterns for defeating setbacks. They can then apply the lessons in their personal and professional lives.

MY BIGGEST CHALLENGE

The biggest challenge I feel I have overcome so far in my life was:

☛ When I...

....

The things I did to overcome the challenge were:

☛ I...

☛ I...

☛ I...

☛ I...

☛ I...

The things I can do to follow similar principles to tackle a present or future challenge are:

☛ I can..

☛ I can..

☛ I can..

✎ *SUCCESS: MY DAILY DISCIPLINES*

Many people have desires, few embrace the discipline required to achieve their dreams. Running your first London Marathon, for example, calls for following a strict training pattern throughout the preceding year. Peak performers begin by getting the basics rights. Laying the foundation provides the platform for making the best use of their talents. Describe the daily disciplines you must follow to achieve your picture of success.

SUCCESS:
MY DAILY DISCIPLINES

The things I must do each day to reach my goals are:

1) To...

....

....

2) To...

....

....

3) To...

....

....

Two exercises stood out for Leroy: *My Alarm Bell Experiences* and *My Best Team Performance.* Crashing his Ferrari made a massive impact on his life. Previously feeling invulnerable, he confronted reality when climbing from the wreckage. Leroy recoiled from what he saw.

"The front pages of tabloids pictured me standing by the car looking as if I had seen a ghost," he said. "Luckily I did not kill anybody. That was the moment I decided to rebuild my life. My manager dropping me from the team was another 'Alarm Bell' experience that reinforced the decision."

How to recover from these setbacks? Leroy planned to apply the lessons from *My Best Team Performance.* The principles he followed then must become part of his everyday behaviour. Previously he was an outspoken critic of mistakes committed by others. Now he was the outcast. Saying positive things to fellow players, training hard and sacrificing himself would work to the team's advantage. The manager might pick him to play tomorrow, next week or in several months. Leroy felt that, whatever happened, he was now in charge of his destiny. Taking ten minutes by himself, he completed the exercise on *Success: My Daily Disciplines,* then transferred this list to a second paper in his wallet.

THE DELIVERY

Karl Malone, the Utah Jazz basketball star, is called 'The Mail Man'. Why? Because he always delivers. Great athletes give great performances on gre
at occasions. Pursuing the daily disciplines creates the springboard for their success. Greatness, however, calls for producing that 'little bit extra' at critical moments. Making magic may seem spontaneous, but it is often the fruit of honing their 'personal radar'. Great performers see patterns and predict what will happen before it occurs. How to widen your radar and repertoire? People can anticipate potential events. Rehearsing their responses increases the likelihood of choosing the right

strategy and getting the right results.

Leroy was clear about his chosen direction, but what might happen along his journey? What might be the positives? What might be the pitfalls? Unexpected events can throw you off-course. Sometimes it takes days, months or even years to re-centre and get back on track. Leroy was invited to tackle the following exercises that explored what might happen in the next year.

✎ MY FUTURE: THE POSITIVE SCENARIO

Peak performers anticipate events they may experience in the future. Rehearsing responses to things going well is as important as rehearsing responses to things going badly. Why? Success breeds complacency. People show-off or believe the job is already finished. Losing momentum, they wake up too late. The opposing team scores twice to win the match or competitors innovate while you stagnate. This exercise invites you to do two things.

1) Describe a possible positive situation that you may encounter in the next year.

2) Describe the specific things you can do to build on this situation.

Goldminers who hit a seam of gold roll up their sleeves. Gaining the Grail calls for re-doubling their efforts, rather than taking a month's holiday. People can find it helpful to rehearse their response to successes they may encounter in the future.

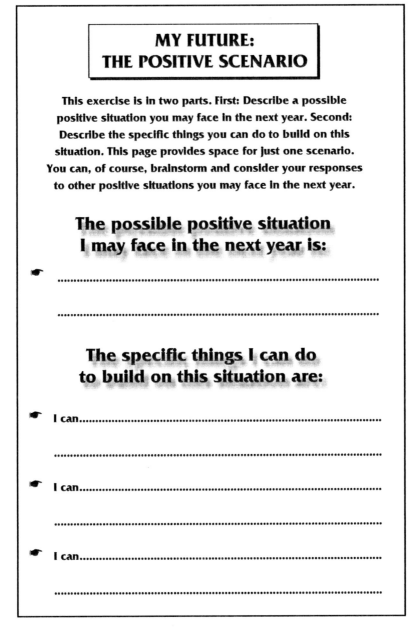

MY FUTURE:
THE POSITIVE SCENARIO

This exercise is in two parts. First: Describe a possible
positive situation you may face in the next year. Second:
Describe the specific things you can do to build on this
situation. This page provides space for just one scenario.
You can, of course, brainstorm and consider your responses
to other positive situations you may face in the next year.

The possible positive situation
I may face in the next year is:

☞ ....

....

The specific things I can do
to build on this situation are:

☞ I can..

....

☞ I can..

....

☞ I can..

....

✎ MY FUTURE: THE STICKY MOMENTS SCENARIO

Time to anticipate potential problems. People who rehearse their repertoire of possible responses to difficulties become positive, rather than feel paralysed. Why? Three reasons: First: They have already got over the shock and been through the 'Change Curve'. Second: They have done lots of pre-work which 'buys them time' to check the actual reality. They can scan the situation to sort out what fits-and does not fit-their anticipated picture. Third: They can become proactive, choose the best option and shape the future reality. This exercise invites you to do two things.

1) Describe a possible difficult situation that you may encounter in the next year.

2) Describe the specific things you can do to manage this situation.

The page provides space for one such sticky moment. You may wish, however, to brainstorm and consider your responses to other difficult situations you can face in the next year.

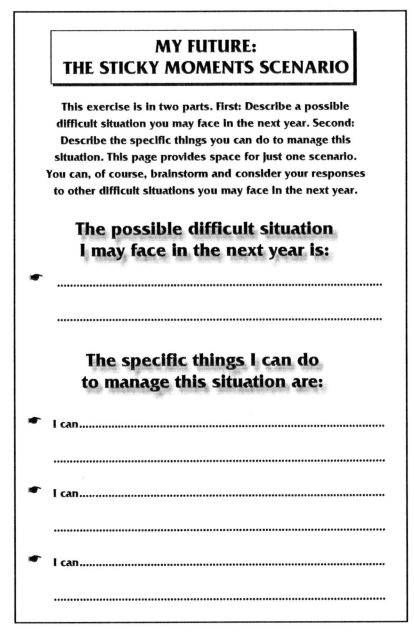

MY FUTURE:
THE STICKY MOMENTS SCENARIO

This exercise is in two parts. First: Describe a possible difficult situation you may face in the next year. Second: Describe the specific things you can do to manage this situation. This page provides space for just one scenario. You can, of course, brainstorm and consider your responses to other difficult situations you may face in the next year.

The possible difficult situation I may face in the next year is:

☞ ....

....

The specific things I can do to manage this situation are:

☞ I can...

....

☞ I can...

....

☞ I can...

....

"Sometimes I lose my nerve during the 'High Noon' encounter with the goalkeeper," said Leroy, choosing a specific sticky moment. "Fans expect me to score when racing through by myself, but it is harder than they think. Years ago I waltzed around the goalkeeper to put the ball into the net. Now I 'think too much' during the one-to-one duels."

"Michael Owen, the England striker, scored a marvellous goal against Argentina in the 1998 World Cup," he continued. "Beating several defenders, he flew past the goalkeeper and shot high into the net. He had no fear. I used to be like that. My manager says he is more likely to pick me if I put myself in scoring positions, even if I miss. So I'd like to look at what to do when I'm running through with the ball."

Pleasure had been replaced by pain, confidence by self-doubt. Conquering this feeling had become a metaphor for Leroy. If he could manage the 'High Noon' situation, he could also take charge of his life. Most of his thinking must be done before going onto the pitch, he could then release his natural talent during the critical moments. He needed to take three steps. First: To choose his strategy. Second: To practice this strategy. Third: To implement the strategy during a match. Leroy listed the options he had when presented with such a goal-scoring opportunity.

THE POSSIBLE OPTIONS WHEN
RACING TOWARDS GOAL ARE:

a) To focus on scoring the goal.

Leroy could take the direct route. Racing past defenders, he could look up and pick his spot in the net. Becoming calm, he could shoot the ball into the goal. Sounds simple, but this is the pattern followed by the best forwards. Glory came from scoring, but what if he failed and the crowd got on his back?

"Fans forgive a lot if you score goals," said Leroy. "Sometimes I'll score, sometimes I'll miss. One international player said: 'The season I finished as the top goal scorer, I also finished as the top goal misser.' That's the attitude I must take onto the pitch."

b) To focus on the goalkeeper.

People sometimes focus on problems, rather than on opportunities. Leroy could look up and concentrate on the goalkeeper. Becoming obsessed by the barrier, he would freeze. Defenders would tackle, win the ball and launch their own attacks. Focusing on the problem would lead to pressure being put on his own team.

c) To dally on the ball and lose the opportunity.

Forwards who lack confidence try to make certain they will score. Presented with a clear path to goal, they take too many touches and lose possession. Leroy was an instinctive soccer player. He must do most of his mental rehearsal before the match. Thinking too much during the game led to inner-doubts and hesitation. He must follow his instinct at critical moments and release his natural talent. His manager frequently implored him to take the direct route, use his pace and "take a gamble in the last third of the field."

d) To double back and try to beat defenders for a second time.

Leroy could revisit his starring role in the school playground. Faced with only the goalkeeper to beat, he showed off by retracing his steps and dribbling past other kids for a second time. Felt great: but he established a pattern of over-elaborating. "Do the simple thing," implored his manager. One problem. He recalled the adrenalin rush of scoring 'the goal of a lifetime' in his debut game. How to compensate? Leroy must replace it with the satisfaction of scoring twenty simple goals a season, his passport to a regular place in the team.

e) To pass responsibility to a team mate.

"After you," says one player, when offered a shooting chance. "No, after you," says another. Leroy could abdicate his responsibility as a goal-scorer and pass to a colleague. Players who go through a bad patch don't want the ball and look for a place to disappear.

"Hiding became a habit for me last season," he admitted, "especially after making mistakes. Professionals know how to disguise their own errors, making them look like their team-mate's fault. Waving your arms around after sending a bad pass, you shout: 'Why didn't you go for the ball?' The crowd backs you, but your fellow pros know what is happening. Some give you a mouthful, other just turn away in the dressing room."

Leroy chose Option A, taking the direct route. Part of his homework would be to spend 15 minutes a day mentally rehearsing scoring when racing through on the goal. Positive thinking was also vital. Scoring 3 times out of 10 must be seen as a 30% Success Rate, not a 70% Failure Rate. What to do if he missed? Leroy could follow the path taken by many athletes and develop some 'Rituals for Re-Centring'.

Sports people repeat certain habits to prepare themselves to perform at their best. Tennis players give 100% to win each point. Before recommencing the game, however, they practice rituals to regain their composure. The server bounces the ball several times. The receiver collects their thoughts and prepares to return the serve. Golfers practice rituals to recompose themselves after missing a putt. Emmanual Petit, the Arsenal midfield player, performs a ritual every time he comes onto the field, recalling his brother who died at a young age. Missing a goal might be embarrassing to Leroy. In the great order of things, however, it wasn't that vital. Part of his homework involved tackling the following exercise for regaining his composure.

✎ *RITUALS FOR RE-CENTRING*

Great performers develop methods to focus on the 'now'. Putting successes and mistakes behind them, they bring a fresh mind to the next task. (Some of these rules are shown below.) This exercise invites you to explore how to prepare yourself to perform at critical times.

1) Describe a specific situation where you sometimes feel the need to re-centre. For example: coping with a key moment in sports, preparing to make a presentation or returning home after a long trip.

2) Describe the specific things you can do to re-centre and prepare to do your best in this situation.

(Teams and organisations also need time to re-centre. People in network organisations, for example, must come together to reassert their common values. Otherwise people just go off and do their own thing. Consider ways that your team or organisation can find ways to re-centre. People are then more likely to focus on their agreed vision and deliver visible results.)

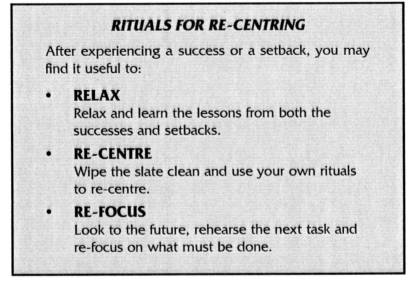

RITUALS FOR RE-CENTRING

After experiencing a success or a setback, you may find it useful to:

• **RELAX**
Relax and learn the lessons from both the successes and setbacks.

• **RE-CENTRE**
Wipe the slate clean and use your own rituals to re-centre.

• **RE-FOCUS**
Look to the future, rehearse the next task and re-focus on what must be done.

RITUALS FOR RE-CENTRING

This exercise invites you to focus on how to prepare yourself to perform at your best at critical times. First: Describe a specific situation where you sometimes feel the need to re-centre. For example: coping with a key moment in sports, preparing to make a presentation or returning home after a long trip. Second: Describe the specific things you can do to re-centre and prepare to do your best in this situation.

The specific situation where I sometimes need to re-centre is:

☞ When..

....

The specific things I can do to re-centre and prepare to do my best in this situation are:

☞ I can..

....

☞ I can..

....

☞ I can..

....

Leroy felt able to overcome missing a goal, but one piece of information was still required if he was to deliver. He must understand his key sponsor's agenda. Why? The manager had the final word on whether or not he won a regular place in the team. "Think like an MD," is the advice given to business people before making a decision. "If you were the MD, what would you do in this situation?" Similar rules apply in sport. Soccer players often focus on their own game and lie in bed at night replaying the missed tackle or goal. Managers like players who take a 'helicopter view' and see the whole team's performance. How to find out what his key sponsor wanted? He could ask him, make clear contracts and fulfil his promises. Leroy must also understand the composition of great teams.

Championship teams have three kinds of contributors. They get the right balance between Controlling, Consistent and Creative performers. Whether they participate in sports, the arts or business, winning teams need:

CONTROLLERS

People who have a positive and inspiring influence. They take charge, set the strategy and provide others with the support they need to do their job. Controlling performers often produce outstanding acts of 'heroism' that makes the difference between winning and losing. They also shape the strategy for the team to achieve ongoing success.

CONSISTENTS

People who do the right thing in the right way every day. Consistent performers *always* ensure the team reaches a certain standard. They are self-managing people who guarantee that the team regularly produces the right results.

CREATIVES

People who provide the imagination needed to make breakthroughs. Creative performers use their talents to think 'out of the box'. They feed off challenges and love to find possible solutions to seemingly impossible problems.

"But I'm a bit of each kind of performer," you may argue. When doing work you love, for example, this will certainly be the case. You will then take Control, do Consistent work and add Creativity. Great teams aim to achieve this ideal of everybody scoring highly in each category. But what if this isn't possible? The solution is to get the right mix of performers in the team.

Championship Teams is an exercise that is normally given to leaders. Leroy spent thirty minutes using it as a framework, however, to discuss the qualities he took onto the field. Applying the lessons would boost his chances of winning a regular place in the team.

✎ CHAMPIONSHIP TEAMS

Imagine you are the leader of your team at work. You need to get the right balance between 'Controllers', 'Consistents' and 'Creatives'. The following exercise invites you to explore five questions.

1) What is the percentage of different contributors to your team?

   Leroy's team had three Controllers, three Consistents and five Creatives. "The balance is wrong," he said. "We either win or lose heavily. We definitely need more consistent players." What is the percentage in your team at work? Do you have the right mix? What would be the perfect balance?

2) How can you encourage the different contributors to give their best to the team?

   Controllers tend to be self-motivated. They enjoy being appreciated by the leader, however, and acknowledged as shaping the team's strategy. Consistents always ensure that the team reaches a certain standard. Leaders must reward their crucial contribution. Creatives like time to talk about their performance. Recognition is vital, but so is showing them how, within parameters, they can channel their talents to serve the team.

Looking at your own team: How can you encourage each type of person to make their best contribution towards achieving the team's targets?

3) How you rate yourself in each of the three categories?

Leroy gave himself the following scores: Controller: 3/10, Consistent 3/10. Creative 9/10. "Great teams have Controllers right down their spine," he said. "Peter Schmeichal, Tony Adams and Alan Shearer are players who radiate confidence. Mark Hughes is one of my role models, because defenders feel unnerved by his presence. Taking a leaf out of his book, I must dominate my part of the field. Consistency is also required if I am to keep my place in the team."

4) How can you improve your performance in each of the three categories?

Leroy revisited what he wrote during the exercise on *My Best Team Performance*. What did he do right during that match? He encouraged his colleagues, ran to receive the ball from defence and kept trying for 90 minutes. Leroy must demonstrate similar behaviour in every match to keep his place throughout the season.

5) What are the specific steps you can take to get the right balance of contributors in your team?

Leaders are paid to build a winning team today, but they must also keep an eye on tomorrow. The first step is to get the right balance and quickly deliver success. Failure to achieve results means getting the sack. The second step is to find the next generation of Controllers, Consistents and Creatives. The third step is to integrate these people into the set-up and lay the foundations for producing ongoing success.

Have you got the right balance in your team? Do you have to recruit certain types of people or can you develop them from within? Describe how you can recruit, reward and retain the people who will build a winning team.

CHAMPIONSHIP TEAMS:
THE DIFFERENT TYPES OF CONTRIBUTORS

Championship teams get the right balance between three types of performers: 'Controllers', 'Consistents' and 'Creatives'. One key point. Such people have a positive attitude and influence. Those who have a negative influence do not contribute to the team.

The following exercises invite you to do five things. First: To consider the percentage of different contributors to your team. Second: To identify how to encourage the different contributors to give their best to the team. Third: To rate yourself in each of these areas of contribution. Fourth: To identify specific things you can do to improve in each area of contribution. Five: To identify specific things you can do to get the right balance of contributors in your team.

TEAM %

Controllers

Consistents

Creatives

CHAMPIONSHIP TEAMS: ENCOURAGING THE CONTRIBUTORS

Controllers

The specific things we can do to encourage controllers to make their best contribution

☞ ....

☞ ....

☞ ....

Consistents

The specific things we can do to encourage consistents to make their best contribution

☞ ....

☞ ....

☞ ....

Creatives

The specific things we can do to encourage creatives to make their best contribution

☞ ....

☞ ....

☞ ....

CHAMPIONSHIP TEAMS:
RATING MY OWN CONTRIBUTION

"But I'm a bit of each type," you may argue. This is almost certainly the case. When doing something you enjoy, for example, you may take Control, do Consistent work and add Creativity. The following two pages ask you to do two things. First: To rate yourself as each type of contributor to the team. Rate this on a scale 0-10. Second: To identify specific things you can do to improve each type of contribution.

0-10

Controlling

Rate your contribution to the team as a Controlling Performer. Somebody who is positive and inspiring. Somebody who takes charge, sets the strategy and provides others with the support they need to do their job. Do this on a scale 0-10.

Consistent

Rate your contribution to the team as a Consistent Performer. Somebody who does the right thing in the right way every day. Do this on a scale 0-10.

Creative

Rate your contribution to the team as a Creative Performer. Somebody who uses their talents to find 'out of the box' ways to help the team to reach its goals. Do this on a scale 0-10.

CHAMPIONSHIP TEAMS: IMPROVING MY CONTRIBUTION

Controlling

**The concrete things I can do to
improve as a controlling performer are:**

☞ I can...

☞ I can...

☞ I can...

Consistent

**The concrete things I can do to
improve as a consistent performer are:**

☞ I can...

☞ I can...

☞ I can...

Creative

**The concrete things I can do to
improve as a creative performer are:**

☞ I can...

☞ I can...

☞ I can...

CHAMPIONSHIP TEAMS:
THE DIFFERENT TYPES OF CONTRIBUTORS

Championship teams are continually looking to improve. Have you got the right balance of Controllers, Consistents and Creatives? Do you have to recruit certain types of people or can you develop them from within the team? Describe the practical steps you can take to recruit, reward and retain the contributors who will help you to build a successful team.

The specific steps we can take to make sure we get the right balance of contributors to our team are:

☞ To...

....

☞ To...

....

☞ To...

....

☞ To...

....

☞ To...

....

THE DESTINATION

Time to come down to earth. Leroy aimed to develop a commanding presence on the field, but he must now translate his intentions into reality. Zen-like philosophies such as: "The journey is the destination," did not appeal to him. He preferred his captain's motto of: "Take one day at a time." Professional soccer players' lives are organised from an early age. Discarding this 'outer discipline' and relearning 'inner discipline' can be difficult. Leroy's best chance lay in creating a specific action plan. Re-centering was also important, so he looked back at the original goals written during the first exercise on *Success*. Did his answers still ring true?

"I stand by every word I wrote," he said. "My mind is made up. Being a good father remains the top priority, followed by being a good professional. Soccer is the world I know best, so this will be the easiest part to tackle. I'm also keen to improve my relationship with my ex-wife. Clare has known me for years and is the only woman who keeps my feet on the ground. Frequently in the past I let her down by getting drunk or throwing away money. Fed-up with mothering me, she finally moved out. My aim is to focus on what's best for our son. One day we might get around to rebuilding our marriage."

"My fear has been filling the 'dead time' in the afternoon," continued Leroy. "Previously I spent the time after training drinking or gambling. Extra ball-work with the coach is a possibility, but so is doing voluntary work with local teenagers. The club is going back to grass roots and rebuilding it's links with the community, so the manager would approve. Ironic, isn't it? I've spent years living on the edge. Now I want to be a good role model for young people. Seeing my picture in the paper after the car crash was the turning point. Staring disaster in the face taught me that being a good professional is the only option. The alternative is to throw away my career."

Actions speak louder than words. Leroy tackled the following exercise that focused on the specific steps he could take towards reaching his goals. Particular attention was paid to getting some 'early wins'.

✎ SUCCESS: MY ACTION PLAN

Daily life comes down to getting the right balance between philosophies and practicalities. Grand designs are fine, but turning them into reality calls for attention to detail. This exercise is in three parts.

1) Describe the three main goals you want to achieve to fulfil your picture of success.

2) Describe the practical things you can do to reach each of these three main goals.

3) Describe the probability of you reaching each of the main goals. Do this on a scale 0-10.

SUCCESS:
MY ACTION PLAN

I want to:

1) ....

☞ ....

☞ ....

☞ ....

The probability of me doing these things is:........................../10

2) ....

☞ ....

☞ ....

☞ ....

The probability of me doing these things is:........................../10

3) ....

☞ ....

☞ ....

☞ ....

The probability of me doing these things is:........................../10

Athletes write training schedules for competing in certain events. Aiming to run 9.8 in the 100 Meters final at the Sydney Games in 2000, for example, an Olympic sprinter follows check lists, such as: Monday January 4, 1999: run 5 miles; do 50 press-ups; etc. Leroy applied the same discipline to developing good habits in his daily life. For example:

I WANT TO:

1) Be A Good Father.

- Walk my son to school at 8.30 in morning before going to training. (He lives just round the corner, but previously I have left this to my ex-wife who takes part in the school run.)

- Take him to see Manchester United, his favourite team, twice in the next three months. Will arrange this with a friend who can drive us to Old Trafford.

- Spend every Sunday with my son and, if she is willing, my ex-wife. Spend quality time together with them, rather than watch soccer on Sky Television.

- The probability of me doing these things is: 8/10

2) Be A Good Professional.

- Meet the manager next week to report back from today's session. Determine what I must do to win a regular place in the first team. Set personal goals for doing these things, both in training and in matches. Write these goals and look at them twice a day.

- Repeat what I did during my best team performance: encourage my team-mates, run to receive the ball and sweat for 90 minutes.

- Run into scoring positions at least 10 times during a game. Be calm, focus on the goal and try to shoot into the net. Re-gather my composure and continue with the game.

• The probability of me doing these things is: 9/10

3) Be A Good Model For Young People And Give Something Back To The Community.

- Run soccer coaching sessions in the afternoons for local teenagers. Volunteer for this tomorrow. Do my first session within the next month.

- Visit schools to talk about the dangers of getting involved with drink and gambling. Check with the club's Communication's Director that this is okay. Meet my Probation Officer to arrange the visits to schools.

- Go on local radio to share my experiences as a warning to listeners. Check with the club that this is okay. Ring the soccer reporter to fix a date for doing the radio programme.

• The probability of me doing these things is: 8/10

Athletes 'work in curves': sometimes their form goes up, sometimes their form goes down. The Holy Grail is to reach the top of the curve and break through into the 'zone' of peak performance. Desire and discipline are key ingredients in reaching this destination. Mission accomplished, people may then start to dip. How to avoid falling into a downward spiral? Great athletes re-centre and re-focus on the daily habits needed to achieve their targets. Stardom convinces some athletes they have 'made it'. Refusing to sweat, they court disaster and throw away their careers.

Leroy aimed to maintain the 'upward curve' in both his personal and professional life. Disappointment might accompany his journey, but sticking to his disciplines was the only way up. Building a new set of habits takes at least one year. Going into the future with open eyes, Leroy was prepared to pay the price. How to get some early wins?

"Tonight I will ring Clare to ask if I can take our son to school tomorrow," he said. "She won't refuse, because she has already asked if I can help with the school run. Tonight I will also ring my manager to set-up a meeting. Tomorrow I will practice some 'High Noon' encounters with the goalkeeper. I will count the goals I score, not the ones I miss."

POSTSCRIPT

Success followed quickly. Religiously following his action plan, Leroy did the simple things over the next three months. Winning back his place in the first team, he took his son to watch Manchester United and won praise for coaching local teenagers. Good intentions then almost led to his downfall. Tempted by a lucrative signing-on fee, and the chance to buy a dream house for his parents, he was transferred to a foreign club. Living in hotels proved disastrous. He spent hours talking on the telephone to his former wife and old club captain. "Never go back," they say in sport, but he broke this rule. Returning to his former club, he regained his speed and scored goals regularly. Frightened by yet another 'Alarm Bell' experience, he now swears by taking one day at a time. Leroy has relearned to be positive. He keeps his eye on the goal, not on the goalkeeper.

SUNRISE CONSULTING: CHARTING THE PATH TO FUTURE SUCCESS

Sunrise Consulting specialises in working with companies that are Pacesetters. It helps firms to take the lead, maintain the lead and extend the lead. Nick, Sue and Dave started the business in the early Seventies. Distance Learning materials provided their main money earner in the early days, but they soon began conducting Strategic Workshops. They now specialise in equipping people to manage changes in the future world of work. Sunrise promotes this offering under the banner of 'The Self-Managing Company'.

"£500,000 in the bank provides security, but we now stand at the cross-roads," explained Nick, setting the scene in a telephone conversation. "Sue, Dave and I are still the Compass Setters for the company, so our six support staff expect us to set the overall direction. Each of us is approaching 50, however, which changes one's priorities. Sunrise makes a living helping people to take charge of their lives. Now it's time to take our own medicine. Growing the business is one option, but it may not match our personal agendas. Can you help us to clarify the future strategy for Sunrise?"

How to use the Mentoring Model with teams? This chapter shows one way to apply the principles. As with all creative work, however, it is best to integrate the parts you like with your own style for helping people to achieve their goals.

CHALLENGES

Nick and I met one week later to discuss the challenges facing Sunrise's founders. Stressing he had full authority from Sue and Dave, he started by painting a picture of the company's offering to customers.

"Sunrise works with firms who see themselves at the leading edge. The philosophy underpinning our work is simple: 'Self-management is the key to future success.' Why? Change is happening at the speed of life rather than the speed of theory. Managers must spend their time managing 'Tomorrow's Business' rather than managing 'Today's Business'. They can no longer take the role of being 'parents' or 'police'. How to ensure the necessary daily tasks get completed? The only way is to employ self-managing people who make their best contribution towards achieving the firm's goals. Sunrise equips executives, managers and front line staff to build 'The Self-Managing Company'."

Business was booming, but the founders felt torn. Traditional industries were now beating a path to their door. Sue, for example, had recently been invited to work with two senior teams in the motor industry. Manufacturing companies were also interested in the concept of self-management. Sunrise had the opportunity to massively expand its business: but was it worth the price? Nick, Sue and Dave advised clients to get the right balance between their personal and professional life. 'Physician, heal thyself,' was the relevant principle. Practising what they preached called for spending more time at home, rather than living out of a suitcase. How to find a solution?

"Let's start from your destination," I suggested. "What do you, Sue and Dave find fulfilling? What do you want to be doing in three years time? What are your personal and professional agendas? Everybody has certain life-themes. Nobody can predict their exact circumstances in X years, but they can identify the themes they want to be pursuing. Describe your perfect future. Starting from this framework, we can explore the many different possibilities."

Nick came armed with his colleague's answers. Anticipating the question, they had met two days earlier to share their personal agendas. The start-up years were dominated by bottom-line figures; nowadays they focused on stimulating projects. Sunrise had become a mature business. The founders had also re-found their purpose: they wanted to pass-on their knowledge to motivated people. Looking three, four or five years into the future made no difference. Regardless of time frame, Nick, Sue and Dave said:

WE WANT:

1) To be doing work we find satisfying. Why? Because this is the only way each of us can walk to work with a spring in our step.

2) To be spreading our knowledge about self-management. Why? Because we want as many people as possible to take charge of their lives.

3) To be adding around £100k a year to the £500k we already have 'in the bank'. Why? Because this feels good and gives us the chance to move on if we wish.

"Sounds like you are a long way down the road," I said to Nick. "At the risk of teaching Granny, I'd like you to tackle some homework before our meeting. Sunrise's founders face the challenge of achieving their picture of perfection. Start by considering the choices for tackling this challenge. Continue by describing the consequences of pursuing these options. Finally, rate the attractiveness of each route. Do this on a scale 0-10. Meeting in two week's time, we well then consider the possible creative solutions. If you wish, use the Group Mentoring Model for clarifying your potential strategies. Is that okay?"

(The Group Mentoring Model is described on the next 4 pages.)

✎ GROUP MENTORING

This exercise invites people to share their know-how to find possible solutions to challenges. Start by appointing a Chair Person. It is their job to guide people through the Five C Model. The group then goes through the following steps.

- People select a Challenge they would like to tackle: "How to..." They spend a lot of time clarifying the Challenge. They need to ask: "What is the real result we want to achieve?" It is vital they get an agreed picture of the 'What?' before moving onto the 'How?'

- People brainstorm the possible Choices for tackling the challenge. They then flesh these out in more detail. People can do this by either: a) Working together in the big group or; b) Working in smaller groups to consider the different options. They also list the Consequences of pursuing each route.

- People return to the big group to share the possible options for tackling the challenge. They also describe the Consequences.

- People can gauge the feeling in the group by, if they wish, rating the attractiveness of each option. They do this on a scale 0-10.

- People look for possible Creative Solutions. They need to be imaginative and explore all possibilities. People then choose what they believe is the best option – or options – for them to pursue.

- People finish by focusing on their Conclusions. One possibility, for example, is agreeing on the Concrete Actions they wish to take to tackle the challenge.

The following pages provide a road-map you can use when practising Group Mentoring.

GROUP MENTORING

The Challenge

The specific challenge we want to tackle is:

☛ How to..

....

The Choices

The possible options for tackling the challenge are:

a) To...

....

....

b) To...

....

....

c) To...

....

....

The Consequences

The pluses and minuses of each of these options are:

OPTION A: To..

Pluses	Minuses
☞	☞ ....
☞	☞ ....
☞	☞ ....

OPTION B: To..

Pluses	Minuses
☞	☞ ....
☞	☞ ....
☞	☞ ....

OPTION C: To..

Pluses	Minuses
☞	☞ ....
☞	☞ ....
☞	☞ ....

The Creative Solutions

The possible creative solutions are:

☛ To...

....

☛ To...

....

☛ To...

....

The Conclusions

**The chosen option we want to pursue – and
the concrete actions to take – are:**

☛ To...

....

☛ To...

....

☛ To...

....

CHOICES AND CONSEQUENCES

Nick telephoned the afternoon before I was due to meet Sunrise's founders.

"You may soon find yourself out of a job," he joked, "because I think we have solved the problem. But Sue, Dave and I still want to get your opinion, in case we have overlooked any stumbling blocks. Looking forward to seeing you at 8.30 tomorrow morning."

Meeting for breakfast, Sunrise's founders outlined some ideas they had discarded. Turnover could be increased by buying another training company. 'Too risky', was the conclusion. 'Values-fit' was the key issue in such ventures, as was management time devoted to achieving maximum synergy. What about partnering a company whose products complemented those offered by Sunrise? Similar reservations made this untenable. Moving to the seminar room, Nick, Sue and Dave took turns to present the possible choices for achieving their picture of perfection.

The STATUS QUO Option

Customers were knocking at the door, so there was little need to be proactive. Nick, Sue and Dave had masses of work. Traditional industries were now discovering the merits of self-management. The next six months called for customising Distance Learning, running training programmes and conducting Strategic Workshops.

Pluses: Money in the bank. Varied work. Stimulating challenges from clients in different sectors.

Minuses: Reactive rather than proactive. Sunrise being 'all things to all people', therefore not focusing on a market niche. 'Persuading' uncommitted participants on training programmes to consider the benefits of self-management. Lots of travelling and overnight stays in hotels. Little time to spend with partners and families. Life balance destroyed. Question: How many years do we want to maintain the same pace?

Attractiveness Rating: 6/10

The SATISFYING WORK Option

Sunrise to focus on its strengths. Nick, Sue and Dave enjoyed working with leading edge businesses that embraced lifelong learning and self-management. Traditional industries had also invited them to run Strategic Workshops, but they found these exhausting. Why? "The Directors just don't get it," said Nick. "Macho management still rules. They think they can bully people into taking responsibility. I usually end up with a headache after two days with old style executives." Sunrise's founders preferred to perform fulfilling work with Pacesetting companies.

Pluses: Stimulating clients. Doing work they loved. Capitalising on the growing market for self-management. Becoming experts in their chosen field. The challenge to keep learning and 'stay ahead of the game'. Opportunities to spend more time at home, especially when developing new know-how. The joy of working with people who 'Get It.'

Minuses: More a series of questions rather than negatives. How to open doors to get enough customers? How to charge enough money? How to maintain variety without becoming too specialised?

Attractiveness Rating: 9/10

The SUPER-GROWTH Option

Hire three sales people and four extra consultants. Boost profits from 10% to 20% a year. Target the leading edge companies who like the concept of self-management. Time frame? Probably two years, rather than one year. Realistically it would take this length of time to get the new people selling and delivering their targets.

Pluses: Massively increased profits. Reduction in the number of years before Nick, Sue and Dave could 'retire'. Breakthroughs in reaching new customers. New blood coming into the company.

Minuses: Difficult to recruit the right people with the right values. Time to be set aside for coaching the new people. Nick, Sue and Dave may therefore need to spend time out of the market. Employing more people leads to more people problems. Is it worth the management time and effort?

Attractiveness Rating: 7/10

The SELLING KNOW-HOW Option

Sunrise to learn how to sell know-how more profitably. Why? Traditional consultants often charged clients on the basis of the time spent 'on the job', such as running workshops. Clients now demand increased customisation and the transfer of know-how. Sunrise to put a higher – and more realistic – price on the knowledge it passes on to clients.

Pluses: Nick, Sue and Dave to spend time doing what they love: creating know-how. The challenge of delivering leading edge material to demanding clients. Increased profits. Better life-balance.

Minuses: Finding a formula for selling the know-how.

Attractiveness Rating: 9/10

The SELL-OFF Option

Nick, Sue and Dave to sell Sunrise. Several offers lay on the table, but they had always been reluctant. Potential buyers carried 'Golden Handcuffs', demanding the founders run the business for several years. A massive offer, however, might be tempting.

Pluses: A big pay day. Sunrise to get the opportunity to work under the banner of a larger company, therefore reaching more potential customers. Nick, Sue and Dave to 'retire' early.

Minuses: Difficult to find a buyer who shared their values. Golden Handcuffs. Sunrise's founders required to stay until they hit certain financial targets. Loss of control. The chore of having to report to financial masters.

Attractiveness Rating: 6/10

CREATIVE SOLUTIONS

"Looking at each option in turn, we asked two questions," said Nick, "'What are the best parts of each road? How can we get the right balance between finance and fulfilment?' The problem then solved itself on the spot. Bearing in mind the Ratings, we began by focusing on our two favourite routes: 'Satisfying Work' and 'Selling Know-How'. Next we added several ideas from 'Super Growth'. The 'Status Quo' and 'Sell-Off' were rejected."

Nick, Sue and Dave described the new road they wanted to follow. They felt it provided the right balance between pursuing their mission and paying their mortgage.

The Best Parts From Each Option Are:

a) To do satisfying work.

Sunrise believes in helping people to take charge of their lives. How to practice what it preaches? Nick, Sue and Dave prefer to concentrate on doing work they enjoy. They like doing two things:

1) Creating customised material for Distance Learning.

2) Conducting Strategic Workshops for intelligent companies.

They must integrate travelling to win key decision-makers with spending more time at home writing. Sunrise's founders must get the right balance between creativity and commerce.

"We must relearn to live off our wits," explained Sue. "Success has led us to become too institutionalised. Like our clients, we must start to take initiatives. Each year we plan to sit down to share what we will find satisfying to do in the next 18 months. Based on this agenda, we will then create our strategy. Passion and purpose drove us to build Sunrise. Now its time to return to those drivers. The satisfying work approach might even prove to be more profitable."

Sounds fine: but how to balance their personal and professional agendas? This leads to the second theme.

b) To work with Pacesetting companies.

Fulfilment came from being stretched by leading edge companies. Sunrise works best with customers who want to learn, those who 'Get It.' It is not into 'persuasion' or being 'evangelical'. Staying ahead of the game calls for doing several things, however, such as being able:

- To identify the challenges leading edge businesses will be facing in three years time.

- To identify how Sunrise can help these businesses to successfully tackle these challenges.

- To market these ideas today, probably under the banner of the 'Self-Managing Company'.

Nick, Sue and Dave believe in planting seeds in fertile ground. Saying 'Yes' to some companies means saying 'No'

151

to others. Traditional companies are not ruled out, but there is a simple litmus test. The key decision-makers must visibly demonstrate they are committed to lifelong learning. Pacesetting companies stimulate Sunrise to present pioneering ideas, show the benefits and equip their people to be self-managing. How to manage the creative and the commercial aspects of running such a business? This links to the third theme.

c) To find the right way to promote, price and sell Sunrise's know-how.

Marketing and sales are crucial in the quest to reach more Pacesetters. Nick will hire a salesperson who has a track record of selling know-how. Dave will find a PR Agency to raise the company's profile. Sunrise needs to be featured in magazines read by high tech people, such as *Wired*. Television coverage, such as *The Money Programme*, will also be targeted. Pricing their product remains a dilemma. Sue will study best practice from around the world on how to make money from knowledge. How to put the best price on their wisdom?

"Charging the real costs for customisation provides the pathway to profits," explained Sue. "Sometimes we spend 20 days writing a piece of material, but only charge the client for 15 days. Sunrise must put a true price on the work it delivers to customers."

Businesses need to get into a positive circle. Doing good work builds a good reputation that provides the leverage to charge good prices. Nick, Sue and Dave planned to amass a bank of around 30 stimulating companies. They must remain humble, however, because listening and learning remained the key to satisfying the people who purchased their knowledge.

CONCLUSIONS

How to translate wishes into action? Charting the future path is relatively easy, the hard part is to complete the journey. High performers do a few things and do these brilliantly. They are also excellent finishers. Teams have more difficulty in mastering this discipline. Why? More people means more agendas. Superteams are focused teams. People agree on what mountain they are climbing, why they are climbing it and when they will reach the summit. They also agree on the strategies for climbing the mountain. Starting from base camp, they pursue these strategies on a daily basis. Sunrise's founders used the following exercise for clarifying the action plan for reaching their chosen destination.

🖎 SUCCESSFUL STRATEGIES

Peak performers see things in simple terms. They continually concentrate on the actions that will help them to reach their goals. Distractions disjoint other people, however, and throw them off course. This team exercise is in three stages

a) People brainstorm and then agree on: "The Three Key Things We Can Do In The Next Year To Give Ourselves The Greatest Chance Of Success." People can, of course, choose a shorter or longer time frame. When setting up this exercise with a group, you may want to preface it by saying something like:
   "Imagine that it is your money. Your mortgage depends on the business reaching its targets. How would you spend your time? Would you spend it in meetings? Would you spend it on 'nice to do' projects? Would you spend it on customers? Concentrate on the key things you can do to give yourselves the greatest chance of success."

b) People make specific action plans for following each of these strategies. They focus on the actual things they must *do* to achieve success.

c) People translate the words into action by continually focusing on these strategies in their daily work. They make these the basis for all their actions, meetings, newsletters, conferences or whatever. They keep going until they have achieved success. People repeat the process next year.

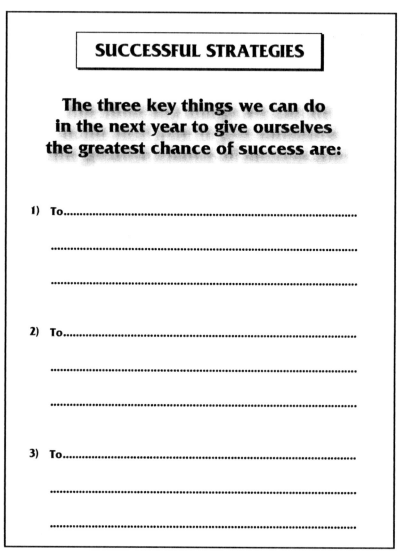

SUCCESSFUL STRATEGIES

The three key things we can do in the next year to give ourselves the greatest chance of success are:

1) To...

....

....

2) To...

....

....

3) To...

....

....

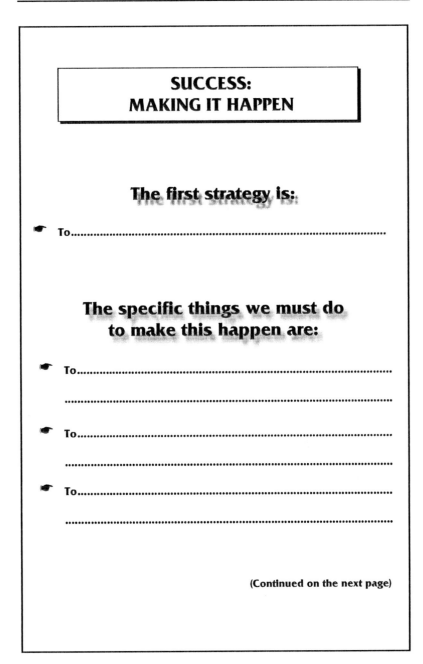

SUCCESS:
MAKING IT HAPPEN

The first strategy is:

☞ To..

The specific things we must do
to make this happen are:

☞ To..

....

☞ To..

....

☞ To..

....

(Continued on the next page)

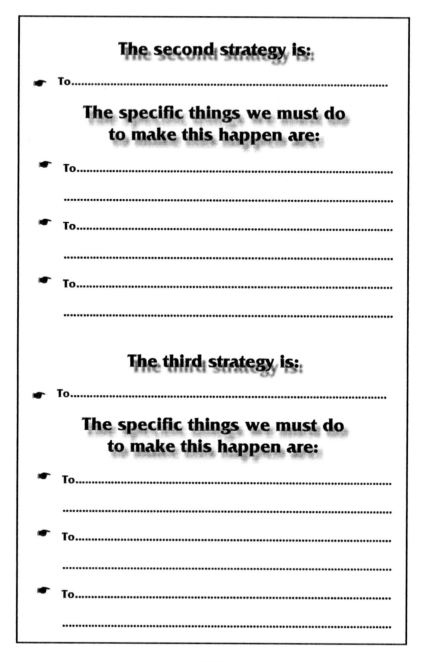

The second strategy is:

☞ To...

The specific things we must do to make this happen are:

☞ To...

....

☞ To...

....

☞ To...

....

The third strategy is:

☞ To...

The specific things we must do to make this happen are:

☞ To...

....

☞ To...

....

☞ To...

....

Sunrise's founders took one hour to complete their action plan. They began by revisiting their original goals. Bearing these in mind, they included some ideas generated during the brainstorm on Creative Solutions. Nick explained the reasoning behind their strategies for success.

"Money is important, but fulfilment must be the springboard for our actions," he declared. "Today we've virtually come full circle. Sages say that you must travel around the world before returning home to see it as if for the first time. People might argue that we could have written these plans before starting the meeting. Maybe: but now all three of us are agreed about the direction and the destination. Although this may sound repetitious, there is now a subtle difference about our second strategy.

The key strategies we want to pursue are:

1) To do satisfying work.

   – To do work that scores at least 8/10 on the satisfaction rating.

   – To do work that gets the right balance between being on the road and writing at home.

   – To do work that stretches us in the area of self-management.

2) To do more in-depth work with a selected number of Pacesetting companies.

   – To each develop a portfolio of five Pacesetting companies with whom we can do in-depth work.

   – To equip their people to be more self-managing which, in turn, will enable these Pacesetting companies to stay ahead of the field.

   – To hire two new people:

a) A salesperson who can sell our know-how to companies, and

b) A consultant who can tailor and deliver the 'classic' self-management modules to companies.

3) To develop new ways to spread our knowledge about self-management.

   - To hire a PR firm that get us regular visibility via television, radio, national newspapers, magazines and conferences.

   - To distribute our Distance Learning packages to Sixth Form Colleges, TECS, MBA Courses and other places of learning.

   - To hire an agency to produce a quarterly newsletter that highlights success stories about self-management.

"The Pacesetters strategy was the breakthrough," explained Nick. "Earlier we discussed massively increasing our portfolio of companies. Sounds logical, but it didn't feel right. Too much like 'old business' paradigms for increasing growth. So we asked ourselves: 'What is the real result we want to achieve?' Sue, Dave and I want to explore new concepts. Expanding our repertoire calls for developing long-term marriages with a few clients, rather than boosting our hit-rate of one night stands. The key is: 'To do more in-depth work with a selected number of Pacesetting companies,' rather than: 'To do work with more companies.' There is a profound difference. One possibility, for example, is to do more fundamental work with our best customers, such as The Telephone Bank."

Sunrise currently partners a leading telephone bank that has exploded onto the market. Sue and Nick initially ran Strategic Workshops for their Senior Team, which in turn led to customising Career Development Materials for their employees. The MD is committed to building a different kind of business. Mirroring Sunrise's ideas, he believes that:

THE SELF-MANAGING COMPANY
IS ONE WHERE:

- The Employer's Role: Is To Show People
  The Picture Of Success.

- The Employee's Role: Is To Show How They
  Want To Contribute To
  That Picture Of Success.

"People have to *want* to work for The Telephone Bank," says the MD. "My role is then to give people the support they need to manage today's business. This gives me the freedom to shape tomorrow's business. Today's employers must create an environment where employees want to commit to the company, make clear contracts and share in the concrete results. People must see that, if they are prepared to sweat, they will reap a tangible reward, such as a monthly profit share. That's what we offer at The Telephone Bank."

The Bank is well down the road toward self-management. Sunrise has influenced the MD's thinking, especially in the area of Career Development. The *Introduction* to the booklet describing their employee's annual 'Career Check', for example, outlines his approach to people taking control of their futures (see opposite). Nick and Sue can build on this good relationship with the company by pitching to help with their Recruitment and Induction. The Telephone Bank looks for three qualities in their employees. It wants people to be:

- Positive
- Professional and
- Problem-Solvers

"Customers who ring us virtually always want to have a problem solved," says the MD. "Time is of the essence to these busy people. They want us to deal with things efficiently and professionally."

THE TELEPHONE BANK:
YOUR ANNUAL CAREER CHECK

Time for your annual 'Career Check'. Many people have an annual physical check to ensure they are staying healthy. Many others have got into the habit of having an annual Career Check. They want to ensure that they are making the best use of their talents for both themselves and their company.

The Telephone Bank believes in encouraging people to take charge of their careers. Two things are vital to bear in mind in the changing world of work. Modern companies realise it is important:

- To encourage people to make the best use of their talents.

- To encourage people to take responsibility for showing how developing their talents can contribute to the future success of the company.

Self-Management is the key to success. Why? Today's world calls for a new kind of 'Trade-off'. Employers take responsibility for providing the climate in which people can grow. They no longer take the role of being 'parents' or 'police', however, when it comes to professional development. Employees now take responsibility for developing their talents. Self-Management also calls for them showing how pursuing a certain route will contribute to the company's future success.

Good luck with your Career Check. We hope it will provide you with the opportunity to explore how to develop your career in a way that is beneficial to both yourself and The Telephone Bank.

The Practice of Mentoring

The Telephone Bank must employ people who have the ability to solve problems. Sunrise can design an interviewing process, probably including simulations, that tests for this quality. The Induction Programme can also equip positive people to be professional and develop their skills as problem-solvers. The Telephone Bank's senior managers must, of course, build a clear message culture. People must have the support and tools to do the job. They also need to know where they can and can't make decisions. Self-management works best in big companies when people have 'Empowerment within Parameters'. Clarity helps them to be creative and produce concrete results.

"The future is in partnering firms such as The Telephone Bank," explained Nick. "Dashing around the country to add 30 companies to our portfolio sounds fine. But the problem is that we might be repeating set pieces and rehashing old models. Sue, Dave and I have each set ourselves the target of doing in-depth work with five leading-edge businesses that want to build The Self-Managing Company."

"The danger is that we miss out on older-style firms that really want to grasp new thinking. How to solve the problem? Reversing our earlier ideas, we will hire one consultant who tailors and delivers the 'classic' self-management modules to such companies. The key is to employ a salesperson who can capitalise on selling our packaged know-how via Train-The-Trainer programmes, Distance Learning materials and CD ROM. But that is another challenge. If I don't watch out, I might say those magic words that people in your business want to hear: 'Can we book you for another half day to find some creative solutions?'"

"Anyway, thank you for today," concluded Nick, as the session drew to a close. "Sometimes it is difficult to take your own medicine. Having an outside facilitator alters our normal dynamics and releases the creative juices. The key from our point of view is that, with help, we have found our own answers. Stubborn characters that we are, rediscovering our purpose makes it more likely that we will be successful. Time for lunch."

POSTSCRIPT

Six months later Nick called to report on Sunrise's progress. They had, for the most part, followed the three strategies. Pacesetting companies proved to be stimulating and led them into new territory. Sarah, the new salesperson was reaching her targets, as was Keith, the new consultant. Events conspired, however, to interrupt their journey. Dave's partner fell ill soon after our meeting, which led to him spending more days at home. Vulnerability is a great teacher. It forces you to revisit your deepest values. A shared sense of sorrow meant everybody at Sunrise began to count what really mattered in their lives.

"Choosing the satisfying work route proved wiser than we might have predicted," said Nick. "Sue and I still serve our customers, while Dave has handed some of his portfolio to Keith. His partner's illness has taught us two lessons. First: To do fulfilling work today, rather than put it off until tomorrow. Second: To plant seeds in fertile ground, rather than try to persuade others to change. Today there are lots of people out there who are hungry to learn. Have you got your diary? Let's fix a date to explore our new challenges. Maybe we can do a deal. Would you like any help with self-management?"

CONCLUSION

One ending brings a new beginning: whether you are conducting a session, running a workshop or writing a book. How can you continue to develop as a mentor? How can you build on your strengths? How can you improve? You may wish to gather stimulating ideas from customers, colleagues and creative writers. Bearing this in mind, the final pages of this book point the way to several writers that provide food for thought.

Today many people are beginning to explore the contribution made by Joseph Campbell. A respected professor, he gained world-wide recognition when interviewed by Bill Moyers on the USA Television series, *The Power of Myth*. Campbell discovered common themes in stories across civilisations. One particular story described 'The Heroic Journey': the quest of a woman or man who tackles a challenge. Campbell's writing is rich in complexity. One interpretation is that the 'heroic person' goes through the following stages to 'Gain the Grail'.

TRAVELLING

Life is plain sailing, but one day you are confronted by a challenge. You get fired, find *ET* in the kitchen or are invited to run a difficult workshop. Do you retreat or go forward? The first reaction may be turn away, but you finally heed the call. The challenge always involves a journey: sometimes outward, sometimes inward. You cross the border into a different world.

THE HEROIC JOURNEY

TRAVELLING

- The call to tackle a challenge
- The turning away from the challenge
- The acceptance and journey to another world

TOILING

- The trials, tests and tribulations
- The search for guidance
- The hard work and sweating

TRANSCENDING

- The gaining of the 'Grail'
- The sense of transcendance
- The return to the normal world

TOILING

Life gets tough. Tests arrive every day, while trials and tribulations obstruct your path. Tempting as it is to return home, you venture further towards the prize. How to find guidance in a confusing world? You gather strength from different sources: from your faith, a person or a book. "The darkest hour may come just before the dawn," you recall, but that provides little consolation. Wisdom and sweat are required for achieving success.

TRANSCENDING

Life becomes magical. Surmounting the final hurdle, you lift the prize. "Near death experiences focus the mind," we are told, but so does gaining the 'Grail'. Standing on the cliff edge, you enjoy a sense of transcendence, seeing life as if for the first time. The clock strikes midnight. Time to return to the normal world. Daily events seem humdrum, but you have changed. Appreciating life's richness, you see the world through different eyes. You look forward to the next call.

Mentoring sessions can follow a similar pattern. Starting out, neither you nor the person has any idea about the eventual outcome. Providing you keep doing things right, however, suddenly things go 'Click'. This can take different forms. The person crosses an emotional Rubicon, settles on a strategy or sees their picture of perfection. Picking up the torch, they implement their action plans. Six months later the person rings to report their success.

Mentors are fortunate. They enjoy the privilege of learning while helping others to solve challenges. Good luck in passing on your wisdom to future generations.

SUGGESTED READING

Normally my books are packed with quotations from other writers. This one has been different. The following pages suggest books that you may find stimulating.

- Bailey, Roy, *How to Empower People at Work*, Management Books 2000, 1995

  Subtitled 'A Guide to Becoming a Green-Fingered Manager', this excellent guide shows readers how to nurture and develop employees, from seedlings to mighty oaks. It includes detailed guidance on the practical counselling skills necessary to truly empower people in the workplace.

- Warren Bennis and Patricia Ward Biederman, *Organizing Genius: The Secrets Of Creative Collaboration*, Nicholas Brealey Publishing, 1997.

  A great book about great groups. Some of the 'take home' lessons are:

  - Great Groups start with great people.
  - Great Groups are full of talented people who can work together.
  - Great Groups make sure the right person has the right job.
  - Great Groups think they are on a mission from God.
  - Great Groups ship; they deliver the goods.

  Today's work places call for people adopting a different approach toward combining their talents. Passion, purpose and peak performance are three characteristics of great groups.

- William Bridges, *Jobshift*, Nicholas Brealey Publishing, 1995.

  "Where can I get a quick overview about changes in the world of work?" somebody asked. "Read *Jobshift*," I replied. "The first 30 pages outline why the 'old world' is collapsing and how the 'new world' is emerging. Better still, it shows how to be successful in this new environment."

  Jobshift gives the big picture. If you find it too theoretical, try the author's latest book *Creating You & Co.* Highly readable with some excellent exercises, it provides a more personal pathway to thriving in a fast changing world.

- David Clutterbuck & David Megginson, *Mentoring in Action*, Kogan Page, 1998.

  The authors outline a number of mentoring schemes, showing both their strengths and weaknesses. David Clutterbuck is well-known as a prolific writer with the ability to set the tone for future developments in business. *Everyone Needs a Mentor*, another of his books, laid the foundation for many mentoring initiatives in both the public and private sector. David Megginson and he are also Directors of the European Mentoring Centre, which can be reached at: 128 Mount Street, London W1Y 5HA.

- Peter Cochrane, *Tips for Time Travellers*, McGraw Hill, 1998.

  "My job, my life, and my mission is to live in the future, to be a pathfinder, at least 5 years ahead of any other human, and 10 years ahead of most," writes the author, head of BT's Research Laboratory. Written in small size chunks, this is the ideal companion to take on a train journey. It shows how people can take charge of the emerging technology and create a positive future.

- Arie de Geus, *The Living Company*, Nicholas Brealey Books, 1997

  Mental Models are both liberating and limiting, says Arie. Why? First: They offer a framework to reassure us that we grasp reality. Second: They blinker our thinking. We see what we believe, rather than believe what we see. Mental rehearsal is also required to chart our path: that way we create a 'Memory of the Future'. So why don't companies foresee events and tackle potentially dangerous problems? Arie suggests five theories as to why they are slow to react. In short, these are:

Theory 1: Managers are stupid
Theory 2: We can only see when a crisis opens our eyes
Theory 3: We can only see what we have already experienced
Theory 4: We cannot see what is emotionally difficult to see
Theory 5: We can only see what is relevant to our view of the future.

A profound book, *The Living Company* shows the holistic way that some business leaders are thinking. Good to know the message, even if you may disagree with some of the conclusions.

* David H. Maister, *True Professionalism*, The Free Press, Simon & Schuster Inc., 1997.

A highly respected adviser to lawyers, accountants and other professional firms, David devotes part of this book to outlining his philosophy of career development. "Few careers are forever," he says, "the choice to be made is not what you want to do with your entire career, but which next challenge would fulfil you (over say a three year period)."

Successful careers often look like a logical progression, as if a grand plan was constructed at the beginning. "Not true," maintains the author. Careers are built by moving from one stimulating job to the next. David concludes: "Choose something that will be exciting and challenging, and will make you happy for maybe the next few years. The longer term will take care of itself." Not the sort of advice one would expect from an adviser to professional firms, but that is why it is refreshing. Well worth reading.

- Larry Spears, Editor, *Insights on Leadership: Service, Stewardship, Spirit and Servant Leadership.* John Wiley & Sons, 1997.

  Servant Leadership was the pioneering book written by Robert Greenleaf. Inspired by his vision, these essays explore the role of the leader as carer, rather than cop. Stephen Covey, Ken Blanchard and Peter Block are a few of the contributors who offer ideas to add to your professional repertoire. *Insights On Leadership* is a lovely book. You can pick it up, read a little and put it down having refreshed the parts that others never reach. Namely, the heart and soul, as well as the head.

- Christopher Vogler, *The Writer's Journey: Mythic Structure For Storytellers & Screenwriters,* Michael Wiese Productions, 1992.

  Employing film-writing as its vehicle, this book pays homage to the legacy of Joseph Campbell, who described the route travelled by people who tackle challenges in life. At heart, says Christopher Vogler, the heroic story is always a journey. He explains:
  "A hero leaves her comfortable, ordinary surroundings to venture into a challenging, unfamiliar world. It may be an outward journey to an actual place: a labyrinth, forest or cave, a strange city or country, a new locale that becomes the arena for her conflict with antagonistic, challenging forces."
  "But there are many stories that take the hero on an inward journey, one of the mind, the heart, the spirit. In any good story the hero grows and changes, making a journey from one way of being to the next: from despair to hope, weakness to strength, folly to wisdom, love to hate, and back again. It's these emotional journeys that hook an audience and make a story worth watching."
  Mentors may witness a similar journey as people tackle challenges, find creative solutions and achieve satisfying conclusions. A superb book.